T0380260

NOTABLE PEOPLE OF COLOR - ST. FRANCISVILLE, LOUISIANA

Photo courtesy of State Library of Louisiana

Dr. Henry L. Hardy

Notable People of Color – St. Francisville, Louisiana
– by Dr. Henry L. Hardy

Researched and edited by
– Tonya Scott Wyandon

AuthorHouse™
1663 Liberty Drive
Bloomington, IN 47403
www.authorhouse.com
Phone: 833-262-8899

This book is printed on acid-free paper.

ISBN: 978-1-6655-7174-6 (sc)
ISBN: 978-1-6655-7175-3 (e)

Library of Congress Control Number: 2022917762

Print information available on the last page.

Published by AuthorHouse 07/10/2023

A special thank you to the following:

Adelman Images, LP and the Adelman Estate for permission granted -West Feliciana Parish, circa 1963. Credits to "Birth of a Voter" by Bob Adelman - CORE pamphlet reprint of Ebony Magazine Article.
A special thank you to Stephen Watt of the Adelman Estate.
Permission granted to reprint the following excerpts: Benjamin E. Mays and Dr. Carter G. Woodson.

authorHOUSE®

This book is dedicated to our great-granddaughter

~Khenzie Alani Magee

Foreword

I would like to first and foremost offer my gratitude to the late Dr. Henry L. Hardy. As trusted editor and researcher for the book: *Notable People of Color – St. Francisville, Louisiana,* I am thrilled to have received the opportunity to assist Dr. Hardy as he shares his contribution with the public.

It was through an uncanny referral that I received Dr. Hardy's manuscript. Imagine two young boys growing up together in a small town. Those two boys were my dad (the late Willie B. *"Scottie"* Scott, Jr.), and Dr. Hardy. Each evolving step these once young boys made toward their manhood was done with a tremendous amount of heart, dignity, and grace. I honor their journey.

Notable People of Color – St. Francisville, Louisiana has a place in history. Dr. Hardy's awareness of the need to share with the world, a true story of the time when ordinary People of Color transitioned to *extraordinary* in our society. Due to their tenacity to persevere with excellence, it was their work which set up generations yet to be seen, to be afforded what Dr. Hardy's generation was not. I would like to take this opportunity to personally thank the portrayed twelve Notable People of Color listed in his book, present and no longer in sight, for their work. I am proud to say that it is because of their accomplishments that I am only one generation removed from what was once impossible. And it is now, for our own children, *everything* is possible.

As many small towns are often overlooked for several reasons, St. Francisville is no exception. One reason is that we are far from cosmopolitan. However, it my opinion that I recognize small southern towns have always been the fundamental foundation which has historically set up multitudes of generations to flourish from those very fertile roots. *Notable People of Color – St. Francisville, Louisiana* now has a seat at the table, along with other published works of the histories of other People of Color everywhere. Everyone has a story, and may all stories, whether oral or written, have a place in history.

And so, I ask all who read *Notable People of Color – St. Francisville, Louisiana* to open their hearts with gratitude to all of the ancestors who came before them, whether you are a Person of Color, or not, as we all came from others who paved the way.

An important acknowledgement to my team who assisted me along the way: Debbie Halprin, my trusted editor and friend who has always been the other side of reason and is always right. Thank you to Leah V. Bennett, professional editor, and longtime best friend for always being accessible. To Melanie Lear of Authorhouse for your grace, Stacie L. V. Davis of St. Francisville, La., for your valuable contribution and support for this project, and Mr. Vincent Smith of St. Francisville, La. for blessing me during my final push.

To my gifted and talented son, Rohan Omar Wyandon, for creating the artwork on the book cover – "you've always had it in you!" To professional artist, Philip D. Louis II, Lauren Hawthorne, and Jarvis Wyandon, thank you for the book cover edits. And to my twin daughters, Raine and Eden Wyandon, I owe you everything times two for the countless amount of technical hours working on this project. The three of you are the light of my Soul. Thank you.

A special thank you to Mrs. Mattie Hardy for your support throughout this process. And finally, to the memory of Dr. Hardy. It was my honor to be of service to you, I shall be eternally grateful.

Lastly, to the divide that exists, may God extend his Grace so that it becomes shortened. Soon and very soon, one day, it shall be no more. And so, it is.

With gratitude,

Tonya Scott Wyandon
Author of *Breaking Into Soul – A Novel*
Granddaughter of the late Willie "Bennet" and Melnor Dunbar Scott, Sr. – St. Francisville, La.

Contents

Dear Khenzie,

At the time of this writing, I am eighty-two years old, and you are a three-year-old. May this book enlighten you of your great-grandfather's life during that period.

I would like to instill in you that the Grace of God and education are the pathways for peace and happiness on this earth. I challenge you to follow in my footsteps and achieve academic excellence and spiritual growth.

In my lifetime, I have lived through periods of segregation, institutional racism, racial unrest, Hurricane Katrina, the first African American president (former President Barack Hussein Obama), COVID -19 (Coronavirus Global Pandemic of 2019), the U.S. Capitol Insurrection of 2021, and the first female and African American Vice President of the United States, Vice President Kamala D. Harris.

My spiritual hero is Jesus Christ. My educational heroes were Professor John Sterling Dawson, Dr. Benjamin E. Mays, and Dr. Carter G. Woodson. Throughout this book, you will find three of my favorite quotes written by Dr. Benjamin E. Mays (1894-1984) and Dr. Carter G. Woodson (1875-1950). May these quotes become embedded in your heart.

Your Great-Grandfather,
Dr. Henry L. Hardy

To Khenzi,

Your Great-Grandfather (my father, Dr. Henry Hardy), had a vision at 1:00 AM in the morning, got up, and started typing on his computer. His vision was filled with hopes and future accomplishments that his great-grandkids might have. Your great-grandfather asked if I could put something together dedicated to you in the book he is presently authoring.

I knew this was not going to be easy as a dedication is usually about a paragraph at most. Well, Khenzi, for me, not sure which paragraphs your great-grandfather would remove, I pondered on this for about a week or two.

The last four years have been a dark hole for many parts of America, well, let's say the world. Dreams for some young adults did not seem to come to fruition. There have been many senseless killings and many wrong injustices. There was so much history I did not know until the last two years (beginning with 2018). Khenzi, in 2008, the United States had its first African American President (former President Barack Hussein Obama), who also became a two-term president. However, succeeding this historic event, in 2016, racism was revealed under the leadership of former President Donald Trump (January 20, 2021) as America witnessed a horrific capital insurrection.

Moving forward, your brother, Rogie III, understands what happened on November 3, 2020. Madam Kamala D. Harris was elected as the first Black/Asian American female Vice President of the United States of America. You, on the other hand, were outside playing with a leaf and chasing your shadow. Your great-grandfather and I have had countless conversations about the safe and amazing childhood my brother and I experienced. Because of this, I really did not know about prejudices or discrimination. As you get older, it is my every intention to make sure you and I have many talks about the "possibilities" in life along with the stumbling blocks that will come across your journey of growing up.

Lovingly, your grandmother,
Pamlynn Hardy

*"We, today, stand on the shoulders of our predecessors who have gone before us.
We, as their successors, must catch the torch of freedom and liberty passed on to us by our ancestors.
We cannot lose in this battle."*

– Benjamin E. Mays
(1894-1984)

Preface

Exclusion of Notable People of Color in West Feliciana Parish

Much has been written about St. Francisville but little to nothing includes the time when St. Francisville consisted of Notable People of Color. My experience in St. Francisville includes the period from 1949 through 1963. It was during this time that I experienced St. Francisville as being primarily People of Color due to segregated neighborhoods. In my memory, I do not recall White people in St. Francisville with the exception of less than a dozen families. Although I do not recall White people within my immediate surroundings, I do, however, recall that more than several of my schoolmates from the parish were of mixed race.

The West Feliciana Parish Census shows that in 1963, the general population was 12,000 of which 68% were Black people, with a breakdown of 8,160 Blacks and 3,849 Whites. Let me tell you what I know. It may be hard for some people to understand that segregation, racism, White supremacy, and White privileges, are forms of cancer that are harmful to a democratic society. Racist actions by some people may be overt or covert, but it is racism just the same. During this time, racism in St. Francisville did not share the true history of St. Francisville. It covered up the many valuable contributions People of Color offered to the State of Louisiana, leading people to believe that People of Color were less capable, and less deserving. It has always been interesting to note that the only African American listed in 'Notable People' from St. Francisville was Derreck Todd Lee (deceased), known as the Baton Rouge Serial killer. Racism hid the bigotry, violence, and theft that led to many White's accomplishments, which during this period, caused White people to believe that they were more capable and deserving than People of Color, hence, the reason for my book.

Part I

The History of the Hardy Family in West Feliciana Parish

My father was Silas Hardy, Sr. born to James Hardy and Clara Hardy of West Feliciana Parish. After living many years in West Feliciana Parish, my father's parents moved to New Orleans. My grandparents, Silas and Clara Hardy had ten children, four boys and six girls including James, Robert, Silas, William, Geneva, Idella, Oveda, Pearl, Rosalee, and Elnora.

My Mother was Elnora Jackson Hardy, born to Iramount Jackson and Julia Ann Percy Jackson of West Feliciana Parish. My grandfather, Iramount Jackson is a descendant of the Wilcox family (White), and my grandmother Julia Ann Percy Jackson (White) is a descendant of the Percy family.

(The following content was provided by my Uncle William Jackson - July 2021):

Iramount Jackson was born to George Wilcox (White) and Marie Jackson (Black) on November 1, 1891. Iramount had two sisters: Isabelle and Corine. Julia Ann Percy was born to Charles Percy (White) and Judy Simpson (Black) on June 1, 1894. Julia Ann Percy had two sisters: Mary and Salena King; and one brother George Kennedy.

Iramount and Julia Ann were united in marriage in 1910. To this union, fourteen children were born. There was a total of five boys and nine girls including Amanda, Mary, Estella, Iramount, Henry, Elnora, Joseph, Julia, Alice, William, Oralee, Louise, Edward, and Marguerite. Pa and Grandma Jane (as they were called by their families and friends) reared their family in an area known as Parker Stock Farm or Old Airport Road, off the road along the old railroad tracks near St. Francisville. The little house near the railroad track was the scene for the birth of thirteen of the children. The youngest, Marguerite, was born in St. Francisville. The family moved from Parker Stock Farm in 1936 to a house on Highway 61 near Hardwood, La. In 1940, the family moved to Elm Park located on Highway 10, which most of us know as "out in the country" where the Jackson family were sharecroppers on a property that was owned by Joseph Rinaudo. In 1948, after Pa passed, the family the family moved from Elm Park to St. Francisville. In the years that followed, the children grew up, got married, moved away, and began to rear families of their own.

Iramount did part-time work for the Illinois Central Railroad (IC) but spent most of his time farming. It is said that Pa used to wear a long jacket year-round with pockets that carried some of the best corn liquor on this side of the Mighty Mississippi River. Pa had a jolly smile on his face, a chuckle in his voice, and a twinkle in his eyes that led one to believe that there were many good memories of untold stories. It was believed that Pa was indeed a man his descendants could love unquestionably. Pa was said to have been a very loving person yet a feisty old soul. He spent a lot of time with his family and did his very best to help rear well-behaved, God-fearing, wholesome children.

Grandma Jane had her hands full trying to take care of Pa and fourteen children. She was a small woman who spoke with a soft whisper of a voice, yet with the fire of an inferno. Once a decision was made, she had a way of letting everyone know she meant business. As head of the family for many years to come, Grandma Jane reared her family and descendants with strong yet loving hands. Grandma Jane was a member of the St. Andrews Baptist Church in St. Francisville where she served as "Mother" of the Church until she became ill and had to move to New Orleans with her daughter, Amanda. Even in illness, Grandma Jane was still the true matriarch of the Jackson Clan. Her love and warmth could be felt when you walked into the room. Everyone recalled the way she would reach out to hug you as soon as she saw you walk into the room. This small woman in size was loved by all that knew her.

Pa died in December 1947, and Grandma Jane died thirty-two years later in December 1979, in New Orleans, La. at Amanda's home.

The Journey of Henry L. Hardy

I was born in 1940. My siblings, Silas, William, Shirley, and I were born in New Orleans. There, we lived at 2503 South Prieur Street but later, our parents moved to West Feliciana Parish in 1949. Since both of my parents were from West Feliciana Parish, we were among relatives on both sides of the family. Moving from New Orleans to St. Francisville was probably one of the best things to happen in my life. Over the years, the area that we lived in became a depressed area filled with crime. After killing several New Orleans policemen years later, my uncle William "Billy" Hardy was killed by New Orleans policemen at the Hardy family house on the corner of South Prieur and Jackson Street.

When I was fourteen years old in 1955, my father, Silas Hardy passed away due to diabetic complications. Prior to his death my father was a carpenter, and my mother worked at Princeville Canning Company. After my father's death times were very difficult, but by the grace of God, my siblings and I remained steadfast in my parents' vision for their children. My siblings, Silas Hardy, Jr. had four children, William Hardy had four children, Shirley Price had three children, and I had two children. My parents Silas and Elnora Hardy had thirteen grandchildren, of which nine obtained college degrees. During my days in St. Francisville, it was instilled in us that the Grace of God and education were the pathways to peace and happiness on this earth. The steadfast vision my parents had for their offspring paid off and we were indeed blessed.

In 1958, I graduated from John S. Dawson and enrolled at Southern University A&M College in Baton Rouge, La. After two years at Southern University, I enlisted in the United States Air Force and was discharged in August of 1963. In 1963, I married Bessie V. Stephens and from this marriage had two children, Louis (deceased) and Pamlynn. In January 1964, I re-enrolled at Southern University and received a Bachelor of Science Degree in Mathematics. After graduation, I was employed as a teacher in Hartford, Connecticut.

After five years in Hartford, Connecticut, I relocated to Pennsylvania where I was employed by Cheyney University as Assistant Professor, Associate Professor, and Professor of Mathematics, respectfully.

Eventually, I was promoted to the positions of Professor of Mathematics, Chairperson of the Mathematics and Computer Science Department, Dean of the College of Science, and Vice Chancellor for Academic Affairs.

Bessie V. Hardy was employed by the Social Security System in Louisiana, Connecticut, and New Jersey. Bessie and I divorced in 1971, and in 1976, I met and married Mattie Hill Malone.

During my tenure at Cheyney University, Mattie Hardy was employed at the University of Pennsylvania in Medical Research. After retiring from the Pennsylvania System of Higher Education in 1994, Mattie and I moved to New Orleans, Louisiana. In the fall of 1994, I served as Professor of Mathematics at Southern University in New Orleans, La, and later, Vice Chancellor for Academic Affairs.

In 2007, we both retired, I, from the Southern University System and Mattie from Louisiana State University (LSU) where she was employed in Medical Research for thirteen years (1994-2007). Relocating in 2007 from New Orleans to LaPlace, La (near New Orleans) was when Mattie exclaimed she had found her dream home.

On August 29, 2005, Hurricane Katrina was a historic Category Five Atlantic Hurricane that caused over 1,800 deaths and $125 billion in damages, particularly in the City of New Orleans and the surrounding areas. Approximately 80% of New Orleans, as well as large tracts of neighboring parishes, were flooded for weeks, if not months. The flooding also destroyed most of New Orleans' transportation and communication facilities, leading to tens of thousands of people who had not evacuated the city before landfall stranded with little or no access to food, shelter, or necessities.

Most of New Orleans East had six feet of floodwater. After receiving five-plus feet of water and losing everything, our home was no longer Mattie's "dream home." An attempt was made to restore our family home, but Mattie's heart was no longer in it. After living for a year in apartments and a Federal Emergency Management Agency (FEMA) trailer, we purchased and settled into a home in LaPlace, Louisiana.

"When you control a man's thinking you do not have to worry about his actions.
You do not have to tell him not to stand here or go yonder. He will find his 'proper place'
and will stay in it. You do not need to send him to the back door. He will go without
being told, in fact, if there is no back door, he will cut one for his special benefit.
His education makes it necessary."

– Dr. Carter G. Woodson
(1875-1950)

Part II

Formal Education for People of Color in West Feliciana

Photo courtesy of Ken Dawson

Notable

Professor John Sterling Dawson

Pioneer in Education

(December 17, 1871 –September 9, 1950)

The amazing story of John S. Dawson and his "Legacy of Education" in West Feliciana Parish began on a Saturday in January 1890. John S. Dawson established the earliest known publicly organized school for Children of Color in the Laurel Hill area of West Feliciana Parish. They called him "Professor," and he single handedly organized the education process at Laurel Hill.

Prior to the Introduction of *"Formal Education for People of Color in West Feliciana Parish,"* the *"Dawson Legacy of Education"* in West Feliciana Parish is shared. Passages of the history of the Earles and Dawson Families *"Let's Trace Our Roots"* was given by Mrs. Lucy Miller, a niece of John Sterling Dawson.

Let's Trace Our Roots:

"Our family, as far back as we can trace it," began with Lucy Arbuthnot (enslaved last name). Lucy was enslaved on Arbuthnot's plantation in Wilkerson County, MS where she gave birth to Charlotte (the daughter of the plantation owner). Lucy perceived having children by a plantation owner as disgraceful. She became determined to get revenge. Fortunately, slavery was abolished before she got that revenge, and she became a free woman. She vowed that she would marry the 'blackest' man in sight, but a 'good' man-and she did - Mr. Sterling Dawson. Sterling Dawson was born in Virginia on January 27, 1840. He was brought to Wilkerson County by his owner.

After their marriage, Sterling accepted Charlotte as his very own daughter and aided Lucy in raising her to be a respectful young woman. Sterling and Lucy had two sons, William Dawson (who died at an early age) and John Sterling Dawson, and one daughter, Mary Dawson.

The History of Charlotte's family

(The history of Charlotte's family will be given first, then the history of the other Dawson children)

Charlotte married Stephen Earles and to this union, ten children were born: Sampson, Lucious, William, Stephen, Edward, Lucy, Irene, Viola, Anna, and Isaac. Two of the children, Irene and Viola died as young girls. Stephen and Charlotte proceeded to raise the remaining eight children in a strict and religious household where hard work and determination were stressed to the maximum. Stephen Earles, a farmer who also worked at the cotton gin, was described by his daughter Anna as being 'a good ole provider.' Anna also talked about a visit she made to see her grandfather, Mr. Arbuthnot who would make requests for his daughter, Charlotte, to visit him as Charlotte frequently declined those invitations. She considered herself the daughter of Mr. John Sterling Dawson and had no interest in Mr. Arbuthnot. Anna also stated that Mr. Arbuthnot did not have a wife. He just had children by various enslaved women on his plantation. When Anna did visit with Mr. Arbuthnot, she reported his adult children were present, attending to his needs during his declining years. She said they called him "papa." Charlotte, however, was very blessed to have found a 'daddy', and a loving 'father' in Mr. Sterling Dawson.

Although Stephen and Charlotte did not receive a formal education, both could read and write, and both had a strong desire to educate their children. At that time, Wilkerson County, MS. provided no schools to educate Black children. Yet, Stephen and Charlotte were so determined to see their children educated that in the spring of 1885, they loaded their family on an ox-wagon and moved to Bayou Sara (St. Francisville, Louisiana located in West Feliciana Parish). Here the children attended grammar school but soon discovered that grammar school was the highest education a Black child could achieve. So again, they were faced with the problem of no school for their children to attend.

Stephen and Charlotte were again determined, and they felt their children's capabilities extended beyond grammar school. During this period, education beyond grammar school was not free. They had very little money, so they had to figure out a way to pay for their children's education. When they discovered that there was a boarding school in Natchez, MS that accepted crops in payment of tuition and boarding, their dreams finally became a reality. Aunt Anna often talked about her father taking wagon loads of sweet potatoes, peanuts, and other produce to Natchez College to pay their fees. Stephen and Charlotte's hard work and determination did not go unrewarded. The accomplishments of their children are as follows:

- Sampson: their oldest son graduated from Natchez College and New Orleans College. He was a schoolteacher and a Methodist Minister. He was district superintendent over the Alexandria District. He served as secretary of the Louisiana Conference from 1925-1926. He pastored many churches in Louisiana until his death.
- Lucious: graduated from Natchez College and taught school. He went to Southern University and received his B. S. degree. He served as principal of the Independent Rosenwald School until his retirement.
- William: graduated from Natchez College and became a mechanic for the railroad company.

- Lucy: (August 10, 1876 - August 2, 1966) graduated from Natchez College but had no desire to teach school. She met Rush Miller at Natchez College, married him, and moved back to Mississippi. Although she did not become a schoolteacher, she sometimes substituted for her husband.
- Anna: graduated from Natchez College. In 1903, she taught school in West Feliciana Parish and later in St. Landry Parish for nine years.
- Stephen: graduated from Natchez College. He worked as a postal employee for many years in South Bend, Indiana.
- Isaac: Passed away prior to having the opportunity to further his education at Natchez College.

The History of Mary's Family

Mary Dawson Henderson was the mother of two daughters: Carrie and Hannah Henderson, and four sons: Arthur, Jake, Samuel, and John Lewis.

The History of John Sterling's Family

John Sterling Dawson was born on December 17, 1871. He later married Corrine Lee. They became the parents of two sons: John Morris and Thomas James; two daughters; Marion Lucy and Brunetta Annette.

John Sterling Dawson had a great desire for an education while his parents gave him support and encouragement. He graduated from Natchez College and received a B.S. degree from Leland College. He attended summer sessions at Southern University and started teaching school at Laurel Hill, La. in a church. The Trustees, school officials, and community were greatly impressed with his service and assisted him with raising money for a school that was named J. S. Dawson Grade School. This building still stands and is used for society meetings in West Feliciana Parish.

"Professor Dawson," as he was known, taught in many communities in West Feliciana Parish and was recognized as a great educator. Afton Villa Church which was once the only High School for Blacks and located in the Bains Community was named in his honor. On July 28, 1947, Professor Dawson retired, closing his career of fifty-eight years in the teaching profession but not without leaving a legacy of all four of his children in the educational system. Professor Dawson died on September 9, 1950.

Sterling and Lucy Dawson had four children and their off-spring gave birth to twenty children. Sterling Dawson died July 14, 1921. Their descendants have grown to include doctors, nurses, ministers, teachers, school administrators, federal employees, journalists, small business owners, beauticians, barbers, secretaries, military servicemen, postal employees, and more. "We are, today, an army of relatives celebrating a proud heritage." quotes Lucy Miller.

John S. Dawson – they called him "Professor"

At that time in Louisiana, in the wake of *Plessy vs. Ferguson* and its "separate but equal" mandate, segregation continued to make education for Black children practically unavailable, even as White school systems were funded and new facilities were constructed. In rural areas like West Feliciana, Baptist Churches provided space for education in one-room buildings at Afton Villa, Elm Park, Sage Hill, and Hollywood. As the 20th century opened, educational opportunities for Black children seemed dim. Rural schools were isolated, just getting to school was difficult. Because most families farmed for a living, children missed school while working on the farm during planting and harvest times. Rural parish school boards were poor, and the rural Black schools were poorer.[6]

They called him *"Professor"* and he single-handedly organized the education process at Laurel Hill. They were lucky to have a two-story, wood-framed building (used also as a Masonic Lodge) that could handle larger classes. Dawson taught the basics and the students learned quickly. Eventually, two assistant teachers were hired, fifteen-year-old Amelia Brown, and Corrine Lee. The students who excelled were also called on to help with instructions.[6]

Under John S. Dawson's leadership for the next thirty years and with the continued support of the community, the Dawson School prospered. His students went on to high school if they could travel to attend McKinley High School in Baton Rouge, the nearest Black high school. Some went to college and through his inspiration became teachers. In the 1930s, John S. Dawson was principal at the Raspberry Baptist Church School and served as Senior Deacon and Sunday School Superintendent in the church.

The school was located off Ferdinand Street behind the present site of the Historical Society Museum. He eventually married Corrine Lee and they had four children: John M. Dawson, Jr. Thomas Dawson, Marion Dawson and Brunetta Dawson. Each became educators like their father, leaving their mark on West Feliciana Parish education.[6]

Formal education in St. Francisville was provided by the John Sterling Dawson family, Ms. Brunetta Dawson, daughter of John S. Dawson, who became the principal of the elementary school in a building across from Raspberry Baptist Church. The grades were kindergarten through sixth grade. After the sixth grade, all Black students in St. Francisville were bussed to Afton Villa middle and high school. The White school in St. Francisville was located in the Pecan Grove area where many other Black children, myself included, could walk from our homes to the White school in less than fifteen minutes, but were unable due to segregation.

John S. Dawson and Corrine Lee Dawson. Image courtesy of Ken Dawson, St. Francisville, La.

Letter by John S. Dawson

A letter written many years ago by Professor John S. Dawson tells the story from the very beginning of his life in West Feliciana Parish, Louisiana.

"My life at Laurel Hill, Louisiana for thirty years. Early in January 1890, I began teaching school at Laurel Hill. On a Saturday evening, I came to Laurel Hill on the train and was met by Mr. John Jones. The Trustee had met and decided that he would board me. Mr. Jones was one of the head members of his Church and Community and was greatly respected. He introduced me to Mr. C. H. Argue, the Country storekeeper and postmaster, who was also a white trustee of the schools. He liked me at first sight and was a staunch supporter and friend during my thirty years as a teacher at Laurel Hill.

Mr. Jones lived three miles from Laurel Hill and as we walked home, I had to stand an examination from him. I knew I had to be on my "P's & Q's", so a good impression was made on him.

It was quite interesting to know how teachers had to meet the public to let them know school was going to open. It was necessary to be present at Church on the Sunday before to announce it and make a talk so the congregation could see me. In those days, the teacher sat on the back seat alone and I could hear the people whispering, "That's the Teacher."

Monday morning could not come fast enough for me. I rose, ate breakfast, started on my journey followed by several children. Before the day was over, I registered about sixty-three children. Before the week was over, one hundred and twenty-five children were registered.

I had to figure out a way to teach this large number of pupils. Among this large number, not more than twenty could read at all. Most of the work was for beginners. The alphabet was taught the old way, forward, backward, and skipping about. When one came to hearing distance of the school, children could be heard reciting their lesions. Some learned very easily, and some were very slow. By the end of the session, some of the beginners were through with the second grade. I selected a Grade-A class from those who exhibited the ability to learn easily. This class would stand by me and come to school regardless of the weather. They were able to help a lot.

The patrons were so interested in their children that they brought them to school in wagons pulled by mules. At the end of four months provided by the school board, patrons would raise money to extend the term to three more months so that the children could make their grades.

As the school grew older, I taught the students songs such as "Yield Not to Temptation", Joyful Will Their Meeting Be", etc. Each morning devotion consisted of songs and the Lord's Prayer. Children would run long distances to be a part of the devotional exercises.

I spent countless hours with the pupils as I was so anxious for them to learn. All students had to cover their lessons if they required additional hours. It was a pleasure for me to observe how well students progressed in Arithmetic, Writing, Geography, Language, and Spelling.

At the end of the term, I would have examinations and a big exhibition that consisted of speeches, dialogues, drills, etc. They were required to learn their parts well to be in the program. It was necessary to build a stage on the outside of the building to accommodate the people. Patrons at times paid $25.00 for a band to come from St. Francisville to add to the program. The exhibition would be at night and during the early part of the evening, students would recite to let their parents and friends hear what they had learned. Large baskets and boxes of food were brought to serve the vast crowds.

Children were dressed pretty to appear on programs. The concerts would be so full of interest and laughter that guests would never grow tired. They looked forward to the next event. When my students reached the seventh grade, they were able to teach in the rural areas. The Superintendent visited the school often and was impressed with the ability of my "A" Class.

The Superintendent told me he wanted to hire two teachers; one was Amelia Brown. He requested that she report to his office that he had a school for her. I was as proud as she was. She was sent to Hickory Grove School. In those days, some women wore long dresses and even though Amelia was only fifteen years old, her mother had to lengthen her dresses so that she would look more like a teacher.

Few schools had two teachers. Since Laurel Hill was such a large school, the Superintendent gave me an assistant teacher. She was Corrine Lee, another one of my "A" Class students. She assisted several terms, after which she was placed in another rural area. Knowing her from her early life in the classroom, felt she would make me a good wife. We decided to marry. She again assisted me until family duties required that she remain at home. Four children were born to us.

I took great interest in the Church and Sunday School. There was a split in the Church which caused a split in the community, but it did not affect my influence with the people. Both sides loved me. The split side built a Church and called it Cedar Grove.

Each Sunday, I taught Sunday school. If I observed any students acting disorderly in Church or Sunday school, I would reprimand him at school on Monday. On Saturday, I would go hunting with patrons and boys that I boarded with.

Lauren Hill was always dear to me. It was there that I developed genuine friendships early in life. Significant accomplishments were made by many of the students I touched and inspired.

John S. Dawson High School

Image courtesy of the John S. Dawson Foundation

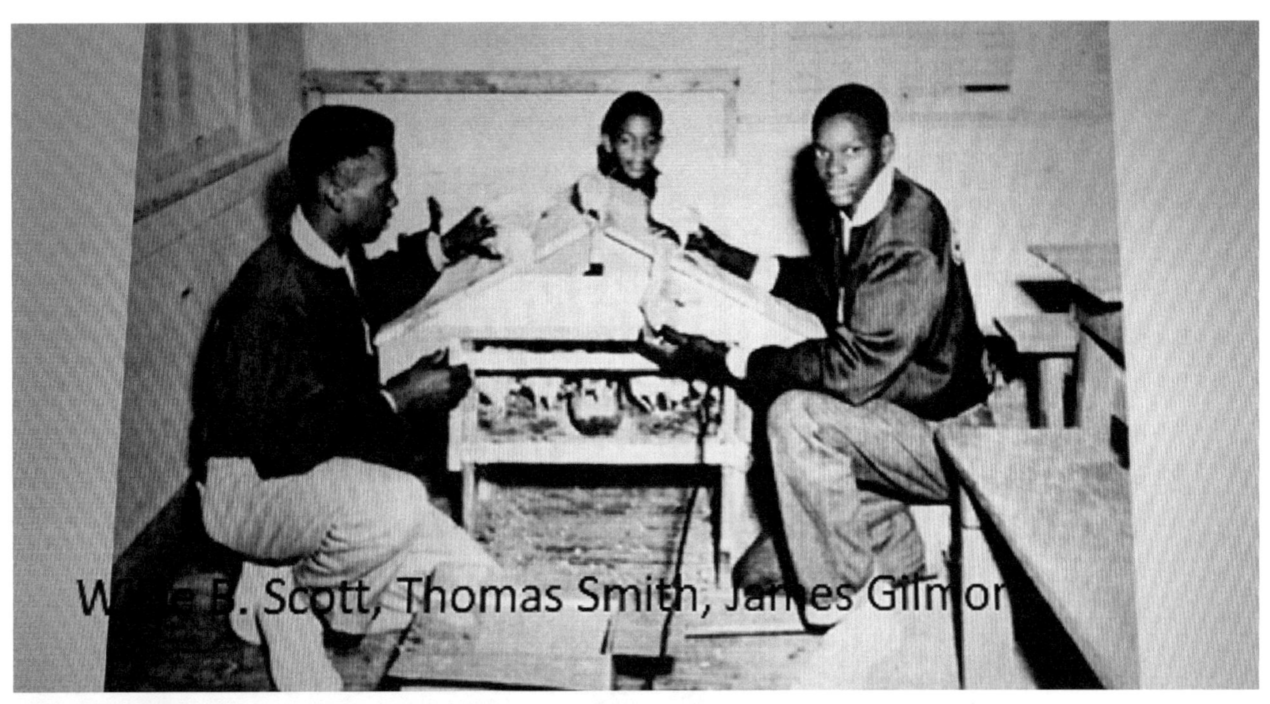

Image courtesy of the John S. Dawson Foundation

Physical Education

Image courtesy of the John S. Dawson Foundation

Image courtesy of the John S. Dawson Foundation

Image courtesy of the John S. Dawson Foundation

Image courtesy of the John S. Dawson Foundation

From left to right: Thomas Dawson, Sr., Tommy Lloyd, unknown, and A.Z. Anderson

Image courtesy of the John S. Dawson Foundation

Principal John M. Dawson with secretary, Mrs. Nixon

John S. Dawson High School

"The opening of the John S. Dawson High School in 1951 was a tremendous advancement of education in West Feliciana Parish. The opening of the Elementary wing for lower grades in 1962 was also significant. It consolidated the elementary education that had previously occurred at the disparate church-based schools into one, new modern facility. The separate gymnasium, band building, home education/industrial arts wing, and agriculture shop further expanded the curriculum and extracurricular capacities of this modern school plant." – unknown

In 1890, John Jones and C. H. Argue brought John Sterling Dawson from Mississippi to West Feliciana Parish to teach Children of Color. Like many other rural Black schools, Laurel Hill only went through the seventh grade. Secondary education for People of Color was slow to develop over the first half of the 20th century. "By 1945, there were eighty Black, four-year high schools in the State of Louisiana, but thirteen parishes were still without approved schools. One of those unapproved was West Feliciana Parish."[6]

Once again John S. Dawson came to the forefront. Planning for a new high school began when John S. Dawson secured land cleared land previously boarded by large trees through a donation to the parish from the Barrow, Richardson, and Nolan families. The thirteen acres of land on Highway 66 was specifically used for a Black high school. This land was used for many sports and other student activities including outside basketball, baseball, physical education classes, fields day, picnics, and more.[6]

John S. Dawson passed away in 1950 at the age of seventy-nine before the new school opened in 1951. His legacy lived on as the school was named in his honor, the John S. Dawson High School. His sons carried on the legacy as John M. Dawson, Jr. was the first principal from 1951 to 1961, and Thomas Dawson served as principal from 1961 to 1969. *(Leland College, Baker Louisiana, n.d.)*

At his funeral, people lined the streets to honor his life and contribution to West Feliciana. The carriage carried him to the Raspberry Baptist Church for the last time. By the effort and dedication of this one man, John Sterling Dawson, many lives were changed, a culture influenced, and a legacy was created.

As time progressed, most of the teachers at John S. Dawson High School were graduates of Southern University A&M and Leland College. Both were located approximately fifteen miles from St. Francisville. Most lived in Scotlandville, or Baton Rouge, rented rooms from families in St. Francisville during the week, and went home on the weekend. The teachers living within the community of the parish with us made for bonding with families. Many occasions, female teachers would take several girls home with them during weekends, extending their sense of community with the students. Regarding discipline, all of the boys in St. Francisville probably got more whippings from principal John Dawson than from parents. "Personally, I don't remember getting whippings from Thomas Dawson, but "Big John" made the difference," recalls Dr. Henry Hardy.

Leland College had a far-reaching impact on the education of Louisiana's People of Color. It was one of four institutions of higher learning for Blacks chartered in the state either during or shortly after Reconstruction. The other three were Southern University (1880), Straight University (1869), and New Orleans University (1873). Southern University began in New Orleans and moved to Baton Rouge in 1914, while the other two were in New Orleans for their entire existence."[10]

Open to all races, Leland College was founded in 1870 as a college for Blacks in New Orleans, La. After the original building burned in 1923, it was relocated near Baker, La., but the school closed in 1960 because of financial difficulties."[3] The 20.9 acres area of the baker campus, comprising four contributing properties and one non-contributing building, was listed on the National Register of Historic Places on November 10, 1982. The college facilities were already derelict at the time of listing. In the early 21st century, only the ruins of the two dormitories can be seen faintly through trees. Frame classroom, the President's House, and concrete classrooms all disappeared at some time."[11] Notable People of Color Alumni Members of Leland College include Dr. Joseph Samuel Clark - President of Southern University, 1914-1938; Eddie Robinson - former Grambling State University head football coach, John W. Joseph - first Black Mayor of Opelousas, Louisiana, and Professor Eugene A Daule.[11]

From left to right: John Jones and C. H. Argue

Image courtesy of Leland College Archieves

John S. Dawson High school provided a diverse curriculum and quality education through the dedicated efforts of the excellent teaching staff. Because of the exemplary education received, many of the Dawson alumni continued to college and have been successful in a wide variety of professions. The diverse curriculum John S. Dawson High School provided included the following subjects: Algebra, American History, Agriculture, Art, Biology, Chemistry, Chorus, English, Geometry, History, Home Economics, Industrial Arts, Louisiana History, Music, Social Studies, Trigonometry, and Vocal and Instrumental studies.

Although there were alumni who vividly recalled some unequal educational disadvantages such as, old textbooks with missing pages which were passed down from the White school, let the record show that students at John S. Dawson High School credit the excellence of their teachers and received a quality education. Concerned teachers, aware about the education of Black students, taught them everything they knew.

John S. Dawson High School alumni include approximately two hundred college graduates. Because of the proximity of West Feliciana Parish to Southern University (thirty miles), a notable number of graduates went to college to become teachers. Thus, the John S. Dawson High School that began in 1951 truly had a profound impact on education for People of Color in this part of Louisiana.

"John S. Dawson High school closed in 1969 following the Supreme Court decision in the *Carter vs West Feliciana Parish School Board* which mandated all the area's schools be desegregated by February 1, 1970. The parish school board chose to reassign the students to other schools and closed John S. Dawson High School. After eighteen years of serving the crucial need of providing modern secondary education to People of Color when it was otherwise unavailable, the school was left abandoned."[6]

"John S. Dawson, the teacher, and visionary, had done his job while creating a legacy for all the citizens of West Feliciana Parish. John S. Dawson High School was vital in its historical role for People of Color in West Feliciana Parish."[6]

"It's not every day you wake up with a mission in your mind, but I had a mission, and I was determined to accomplish it."

– Katherine Johnson
August 1918 – February 2020)

Mathematician & First Woman of Color to work as a NASA Scientist

Photo courtesy of Andrea Nelson-Early

Notable

Dr. Roberta Emery Nelson

Mathematician

(November 3, 1938 – January 30, 1994)

Dr. Roberta Emery Nelson was a native of West Feliciana Parish. Growing up in Wakefield, La. near Rosemond Plantation of St. Francisville, from an early age she demonstrated a love for books and as her brother Lionel Emery recalled, “she was real smart.”

Her parents, James, and Jeanette Sterling Emery were born in West Feliciana Parish. Sharecroppers, they produced everything from cotton to sweet potatoes, and between the two of them were a total of twelve children. To supplement income for the family, her mother, Jeanette, worked to clean the homes of White people while caring for her family, the household, and the farm.

A 1956 graduate of John S. Dawson High School, Dr. Emery-Nelson received a Bachelor of Science degree in Mathematics from Southern University A&M College in 1963 and immediately received her first teaching job at Capital High School in Baton Rouge. Married to James A. Nelson and divorced, with the assistance of her mother, Jeanette, she was responsible for helping to raise her three children: Cassandra, Andrea, and Craig (deceased), independently. Roberta was a practical and conservative woman who had no hesitations about living her life the way she felt necessary. Her educational goals and providing for her children were always at the forefront.

During the summer months, her daughters were able to spend downtime with their grandmother. Her middle child, Andrea Nelson-Early, recalls her mother’s love for higher education and teaching. “My mom actually enjoyed teaching, which resulted in us never staying in one place for too long,” Andrea recalls. “What made my mom *extraordinary* was her natural intelligence in math.” says Andrea.

A trailblazing woman and mother, Roberta relocated her family several times and across several states throughout their developing years while pursuing her dreams. Little did they know, it would be through the educational routes taken by Roberta that would set up a foundation for generations to come. Dr. Roberta Emery Nelson received a total of two master’s degrees in Mathematics from Oklahoma University in 1970, and Indiana University in 1973: and a Doctorate in Mathematics Education from the University of Tennessee in 1978. Accumulating thirty years of teaching experience and fifteen years as a Professor of Mathematics, PhD, with several positions spanning across eight states, Dr. Roberta Emery Nelson truly embodied the hopes of which her ancestors could have only dreamed. All this came to fruition from a daughter who grew up with a love for reading.

Currently, the natural born gift of Dr. Nelson's natural capabilities in math continues through her lineage. Her granddaughter, Faith Early-Cummings holds a MA in Education while her three brothers, Chase Nelson, and Jordan Early boast Mechanical Engineering degrees.

Their eldest brother Jermaine Early, holds an MS in Engineering Management, and previously held a position at NASA Stennis Space Center. Their mother, Andrea, holds a Bachelor of Science in Accounting. Sibling Cassandra A. Nelson, a homemaker by choice, (two of her daughters hold degrees) raised her daughter, Tikera Chisley, to pursue an MA in Education while daughter Spree Chisley-Agbanyim, holds a Doctorate in Pharmacy. Two of Tikera's young adult children, Breiana Square, holds an MBA in Finance. Her brother John Square III hold a Bachelor in both Sociology and Pre-Law.

Both Cassandra and Andrea credit their mom's practical nature as an example in their lives today. As adults, the memory of their mother is a constant reminder that one doesn't have to depend on a traditional social aspect to accomplish their dreams. As Andrea proudly recalls her mom, she acknowledges and recognizes the non-dependent, pioneering spirit of her mom. She continues, "My mom lived her life showing us that whatever you wanted to do, it could be done."

Bio for Notable Dr. Roberta Emery Nelson

- Graduate of John S. Dawson High School – 1958
- Bachelor of Mathematics with honors - Southern University A&M College
- Member of Delta Sigma Theta Sorority, Inc. – Southern University A&M
- Teacher - Capital High School – Baton Rouge, La.
- Master of Mathematics and Instructor - University of Oklahoma, Normand, Ok
- Professor of Mathematics - Columbia Basin College, Paco, WA
- Instructor - Langston University, Langston, OK
- Master of Mathematics and Instructor - University of Indiana, Bloomington, In.
- Instructor - Tuskegee University – Tuskegee, Ala
- Doctor of Mathematics & Professor - The University of Tennessee – Knoxville, Tn
- Professor of Mathematics and Statistics Xavier University, New Orleans, La
- Professor of Mathematics and Director of the Honors Program - Florida A&M University, Tallahassee, Fl.

Notable – Dr. Roberta Emery Nelson

- Professor of Mathematics - Southern University A&M College
- Project Leader for the Metropolitan Transit Authority, Houston, Tx
- Programmer Analyst for Boeing - Richland Operations, Richland, WA
- Member of Times of Refreshing Evangelistic Ministry

“It isn’t more light we need, it isn’t more truth, and it isn’t more scientific data. It is more Christ, more courage, more spiritual insight to act on the light we have.”

– Benjamin E. Mays
(1894-1984)

Part III

The Nathaniel Hawthorne Smith Family in West Feliciana Parish

The Nathaniel Hawthorne Smith Family in West Feliciana Parish

To go from a sweet potato farm in Laurel Hill to Southern University A&M College to becoming Major General in the United States Army, Issac D. Smith may be one of the most incredible and exciting success stories to come out of West Feliciana Parish.

The General's parents were Nathaniel Hawthorne and Sallie Dixon Smith. Nathaniel Smith was from the Laurel Hill area, and Sallie Dixon Smith was from the Hollywood area of West Feliciana. Before becoming sweet potato farmers in 1936, they were cotton farmers. The history of sweet potato farming extended beyond their family history, long before the family purchased their family land on Highway 61. To date, three of the Smith children, including Vincent Smith, live next door to each other on the property their parents purchased in 1948.

Before purchasing their farmland, the Smith family rented the John Barrow property where the first four children were born. Later, on the Douglas Hamilton property, eight additional children were born. The Smith family lived as tenant farmers on both the Barrow and Hamilton properties.

Major General Isaac D. Smith was the third of Smith's twelve children and the oldest son.

Vincent Smith, the seventh child who called his brother I.D., shares the following, "I.D. was always different. He was always studying, reading, or making puzzles for us younger children, giving us problems to work out with a stick on the ground. Anytime we could escape working on the farm or solving I.D.'s problems drawn by a stick on the ground, we would escape way into the back woods where mama couldn't find us. But my brother didn't like to play. He was always serious about everything he did; everything had to be right-just right! Perhaps his personality fit the military life he would later embrace. Amen!" He continued, "We were still little when he was at Southern University, where he was a member of three Reserve Officer Training Corps (ROTC). He never came home; he had to work for Southern University farms at the Agriculture Department to put himself through college. And he helped daddy put Velma through, even though Velma was the oldest sister. He stayed at Southern University year-round, summer and winter. So, I wasn't surprised when he moved up in the military because he was a dedicated man, always was!"

Vincent continued to explain that his parents kept that focus on their children and modeled a strong work ethic, which all the children followed throughout their lives. On the sweet potato farm the Smith parents ran during those days, the work was dawn to dusk six days a week, and still, "if you broke even,

sometimes that was the best you could do," says Vincent. As for Sundays, the family attended church and Sunday school at Rosemond Baptist Church.

Auntie Amelia Brown, however, was Nathaniel H. Smith, Sr.'s maternal aunt. To say she was "highly upon education," Vincent Smith says, "was an understatement." Amelia Brown also happened to be one of John S. Dawson's first teachers in 1903. Ms. Amelia Brown's teaching resume began as a teacher at Hickory Grove in West Feliciana, Leland College in Baker, La., and Tuskegee University in Tuskegee, Alabama. She was also a colleague of the school's founder and educator, Booker T. Washington, the man who later hired her. Major General Isaac D. Smith, again, like many others, attended primary school at Laurel Hill Elementary and later, high school on the grounds of the historic African American Afton Villa Baptist Church on Highway 61 in St. Francisville.

When it came to education, the General's parents provided the same emphasis and resources for their daughters as for their sons. Like I.D., Vincent Smith took part in that effort by remaining in St. Francisville to help his parents with farming.

The history of education for Major General Isaac Smith and his siblings spanned an era of the history of education for Black children. The eldest Smith children either attended Afton Villa or lived in Baton Rouge or New Orleans to further their education. The middle children graduated from Dawson. One of the youngest attended Dawson High and West Feliciana High School when the two schools merged in 1969. The following information on education in the Smith family is as follows:

- Velma Smith graduated from McKinley High School and Southern University and taught at Polk Elementary school in West Feliciana Parish.
- Inez Delores Smith graduated from John S. Dawson High School and Southern University.
- Mary Elizabeth Smith graduated from St. Francisville High School and Southern University. She taught in East and West Feliciana Parish.

- Dorothy Marie Smith graduated from John S. Dawson Highs School and Southern University. Dorothy was also one of the seven first Black students to integrate St. Francisville High. After graduation from Southern University, she moved to California, worked, and retired from AT&T.
- Irma Jean Smith graduated from St. Francisville High School and Southern University. After graduating from Southern University, she moved to California and retired from Los Angeles Power and Light Company.

Major General Isaac Smith and his siblings' education spans an entire history of education for Black children. The eldest of the Smith children either attended Afton Villa or lived in Baton Rouge or New Orleans to further their education. The middle children graduated from Dawson, and one of the youngest attended both Dawson High and West Feliciana High School when the two schools merged in 1969.

All photos with permission of Debra Smith

Notable

Major General Issac D. Smith
United States Army

A natural born leader, Notable Major General Issac D. Smith has always cared about the well-being of others. Married to the late Mildred (Millie) Pierre Smith, they raised two children, Debra and Ron Smith.

Debra recalls family visits to St. Francisville while growing up. "We would mainly visit during the 4th of July or Thanksgiving holiday. And it was a rite of passage for the boys to hunt in the woods with their uncles while the girls stayed home," she shares. "And my dad was tough but never mean. He was also quite funny, with a sense of humor. He loved to dance, and he enjoyed being with his friends and family."

Born May 2, 1932, Major General Isaac D. Smith graduated from Afton Villa School in 1951. At Southern University A&M College, he spent time in the Reserve Officer Training Corps (ROTC) and earned a B.S. degree in Agriculture. He continued his education at Shippensburg University of Pennsylvania where he earned a master's degree in Public Administration. Major General Smith also completed several military educational courses and attended the U.S. Army War College in Cumberland County, PA.[3]

Bio for Notable Major General Issac D. Smith

The wide variety of command and staff positions, varying in levels of importance for Major General Issac D. Smith include:

"Deputy Chief of Staff, Personnel, U.S. Army, Europe and Seventh Army; Deputy Chief of Staff for Operations and Intelligence, Allied Forces Central Europe; Chief, Doctrine and Systems Integration Division, Requirements Directorate, Office of the Deputy Chief of Staff for Operations and Plans, U.S. Army, Washington, D.C.; Chief, Reserve Forces Division, Office of the Assistant Secretary of the Army (Manpower and Reserve Affairs), Washington, D.C.; Commanding General, U.S. Army Second Reserve Officer Training Corps Region, Fort Knox, Kentucky; and Assistant Division Commander, 1st Armored Division, U.S. Army Europe.[3]

"In 1983, when Smith was a Brigadier general, *The Crisis* named him one of the "top blacks in the Armed Forces." At the time, he held the same rank as Colin Powell. He was noted in Blacks in American armed forces: 1776-1983, as well as African American generals and flag officers."[3]

Awards

Notable Major General Smith received "several DOD awards and decorations including the Distinguished Service Medal, the Silver Star, Defense Superior Service Medal, the Legion of Merit (with Oak Leaf Cluster), Bronze Star Medal, the Meritorious Service Medal (with Oak Leaf Cluster), and the Army Commendation Medal (with two Oak Leaf Clusters)".[3]

"In 1999, Smith was named "Rock of the Year" by *The Rocks, Inc*., an association of ROTC officers."[3] "In 2006, Major General Smith, by then, a retired Major General, received a citation from the Louisiana House of Representatives for his service to the United States, which was also passed by the Louisiana Senate".[3]

Major General Smith is honored, along with other African American General Officers, in the African American Smithsonian Museum. He currently resides in San Diego, Ca.

"The struggle for equality in America will not be won in the law courts and legislatures alone. Certainly, we need effective civil rights legislation and the fair interpretation by the courts of constitutional guarantees and rights. But we also require a willingness to assert those rights in the face of bigotry and threats of violence. This article relates how a group of Negroes in a remote Louisiana parish asserted their rights. May their number increase."

– James Farmer
National Director
The Congress of Racial Equality (CORE)

Part IV

When West Feliciana Parish was People of Color
C.O.R.E. 1963

"I know that Garry Winogrand famously said that photographs don't change things. I think that's a very silly thing to say because they do."

– Bob Adelman

The West Feliciana Voter Registration Drive of 1963

During the Freedom Summer of 1963, The Congress of Racial Equality (C.O.R.E.) organized demonstrations in parishes north of Baton Rouge where there were large concentrations of unregistered Blacks. Although the Supreme Court had spoken in the early 1960's, not much had changed regarding rights for People of Color. This is the true story of how a brave community of People of Color, C.O.R.E., volunteers, and others, joined forces to strip away the residuals of racism. Although they were aware their efforts might prove to be dangerous, collectively, they decided that the purpose would be something to risk their lives for, the opportunity to vote. Together, they were able to see the fruits of their labor as their participation changed the landscape of West Feliciana Parish, resulting in the process of overturning the current Jim Crow laws.

The following photographs are from the Bob Adelman Estate. A photographer known for his intimate coverage of the Civil Rights Movement; Adelman forged a career committed to social activism. As the national photographer for the Congress of Racial Equality, Adelman documented the movement in Birmingham and Montgomery in Alabama and the 1963 March on Washington. In 2014 he was named, in essence, a photographer in residence at the Library of Congress.

In the early 60's Adelman began to witness student sit-ins, and with the realization of disturbing treatment of the demonstrators, he went on a Freedom Ride to Maryland, worked with the SNCC (Student Nonviolent Coordinating Committee), and eventually became the national photographer for CORE.

The importance of Adelman's photographs was important. His photography revealed the truth of what exactly went on during demonstrations. His photographs were used as evidence in court cases, to help raise money for the movement and the 1968 Kerner Commission.

Adelman, in the thick of the movement spent time with Rev. Dr. Martin Luther King, Jr. He often noted a few specifics regarding Dr. King. One, was that when he spoke to others, they deserved his full attention, he loved to laugh and that he was a very quiet person. Adelman also acknowledges that Dr. King had a key appreciation of photography, he believed that photographs were key to the movement and that photos revealed the cruelty and mean-spirited nature of segregation. It was in Adelman's opinion that segregation was an organized system of terror, instated and reinforced by the Klan or leaders of communities.

According to Adelman in an interview with Ebony Magazine, the most dangerous thing that happened to him was during Freedom Summer in Louisiana. He recalls the man we will come to know as the first Man of Color to register to vote in the 20th century, Reverend Joe Carter of St. Francisville, La. It was through C.O.R.E., the SNCC and the F.B.I. arrangements to assist the rights of People of Color to try to register to vote upon passing the necessary administered test.

While documenting through his photography, Adelman lived with the Carter family for three days and interviewed the Reverend Carter to learn his story of courage and determination. The realization for Adelman of not being able to vote represented that you were still enslaved. And by voting, it would remove the last badge of slavery.

The following is an excerpt from an article published in Ebony Magazine:

My current view of it is that we fought the last battles of the Civil War. – Adelman

Adelman goes on to recall the night that the Reverend Carter and his neighbors expected the Klan's arrival. The Reverend Carter lived on the end of a dirt road and his neighbors had rifles. He noted although the actual demonstrations and traveling into the town had been nonviolent — once the Reverend returned home at night, he remained steadfast in the right to defend himself and his family.

Approximately only one night after Rev Carter succeeded to vote, the Klan arrived on his dirt road in trucks and bright lights. Once they arrived, the lights turned off and they began shooting their guns up in the air. But on that night, what the Klan did not expect was the volley that happened next. Adelman, now lying on his stomach on the ground near the porch of the Rev Carter's house witnessed the standoff between what he estimated to be over twenty men in the field with guns and this time, they were firing back. There must have been twenty people out in the field there, and they fired back, and there was a gunfight. Afterwards, it was the Klan who quickly retreated. When asked what made the Klan surrender on that night, Adelman answered, "it's because they're not heroes, they're just terrorists."

Notable

Reverend Joseph Carter

Reverend Joseph Carter, the first Black Man to register in West Feliciana Parish since 1902.

(May 5, 1908 - June 11, 1990)

On October 17, 1963, the late Reverend Joseph Carter became the 1st Black to register to vote in West Feliciana parish since 1902. During this period, West Feliciana Parish had a population of 12,000 of which 68% were Black.

The fifty-five-year-old minister arose at 5:30 AM to pray for divine guidance on the day when he would become the first Black in West Feliciana Parish to register to vote in sixty-one years. That morning, he made an announcement to his wife, Wilmeda Carter, that he would be going to the courthouse to register to vote. She was not happy about her husband's decision, and she was concerned about his fate.

After unsuccessfully attempting to register to vote four times, it was during the summer of 1962, the Reverend Carter had his first meeting with the Congress of Racial Equality. He learned the group would conduct several voter registration clinics in an adjacent parish and had sought out C.O.R.E. field secretaries Rudy Lombard and Ronnie Moore. They, along with the FBI would assist the Blacks of West Feliciana by teaching them the importance of voting, show them how to register, help them to understand and not memorize the answers to the questions asked when applying. They promised legal assistance from the U.S. Justice Department and the Reverend Carter accepted, with the exception of not having to take part in any demonstrations.

Fast forward to August 10, 1963, when both the Reverend Carter and the Reverend Rudolph Davis entered the St. Francisville Courthouse to discover they would be denied the right to vote. Instead, the Reverend Carter was handcuffed, arrested, and jailed due the Sheriff's order of disturbing the peace.

The morning of October 17th, the Reverend Carter drove from his home to the Masonic Lodge Hall to gather with forty-two additional other prospective voters. All of them had been attending the C.O.R.E.'s registration clinics, even with the looming threats from White landowners who were warning Black sharecroppers they would be evicted and forced to pay their debts immediately if they sought to register. But the October 17th date was deliberate as most who were sweet potato farmers had sold their crop to the local canners, lessoning the economic reprisals from the White landowners.

A school bus, driven by John Brannon, made the ride to the St. Francisville Courthouse. With about one hundred Whites around the front of the building, they waited. Some sat across the street in front of an iron fence surrounding the now Episcopal Church Cemetery, being called out, cursed at, and taunted.

Escorted into the courthouse by the United States Justice Department, Attorney Frank Dunbar (Civil Rights Division), several FBI agents, Ronnie Moore, and other unidentified C.O.R.E. workers, they accomplished what had not been recorded since 1902.

Circumventing a line of White men, one of whom threatened to emasculate him, the Rev. Joseph Carter entered the courthouse by a side door. At that time, charred remains of a KKK burned cross were still present in front of the nearby office of Aldero Stevenson, a Black businessman.

After producing a driver's license, reading a wall sign to explain the instructions, and taking the test, nineteen minutes later, Reverend Carter returned the cards to the registrar who examined them with his secretary for about sixteen minutes with the secretary saying, "I don't see a damn thing wrong with this." Registrar Harvey objected that only four questions had been answered correctly but the secretary reminded him that the test only required that four questions be answered correctly. "He done passed." she spoke. Reverend Joseph Carter emerged from the courthouse victoriously waving his registration form in the air.[17]

On Friday, October 18, 1963, one day after Rev. Joseph Carter registered, three additional Black men registered: Nathaniel Hawthorne Smith, Ernest Morgan, and Raymond Minor. As Nathaniel Smith came out of the office, Ronnie Moore pinned on him a button reading: "I Am a Registered Voter: Are You?"[17]

It was the Reverend Carter's hope that voting would allow for him the opportunity to purchase land for his family, live on paved roads, and the opportunity to live a better life.

Even with this momentum, that did not stop the looming threat of violence demonstrated on the day Reverend Joseph Carter registered. The violence continued as James Payne, a prospective Black male registrant, was without provocation, assaulted by three White men. James Payne reported that another prospective registrant, Johnnie Hamilton, was told by a White man: "You're enrolled to be killed." This led to windows being shot out while several crosses were burned at the home of Nathaniel Smith, and the Masonic Hall.

The following night after the Reverend registered to vote, several trucks drove behind the farmhouse of his neighbor, bus driver John Brannon. It was after midnight and the men were said to be Klansmen.

They were firing shots in the air and the Rev Carter, who lived at the end of the road and realizing he would have to climb a hill near his house, might end up in a crossfire between himself and his son-in-law. “If they want a fight, we’ll fight,” he explained. “If I have to die, I’d rather die for the right. I value my life even more since I became a registered voter.”[17]

The Reverend Joe Carter practicing test taking skills with C.O.R.E. worker.

Attendees gather in the night at the Masonic Lodge to discuss voter registration.

Johnny Hamilton, Raymond Minor, Rev. Joe Carter and other unidentified men listen with intent.

An unidentified man and woman review voter registration forms.
West Feliciana Parish, La.

All photographs @2022 Bob Adelman Estate. All rights reserved. Circa 1963.

From left to right: Vincent Smith, Mimi Feingold, Phillip Stewart, and Maria Baker. Joining the flock, West Feliciana Parish, Louisiana. 1963 "In West Feliciana, an overwhelmingly black parish where no person of color had voted in the 20th century, volunteer Mimi Feingold urged members of a church congregation to try to vote. She then joined hands with them to sing, "This Little Light of Mine."

Vincent Smith prepares to defend his family after the voter registration. Three days later, Vincent Smith voted for the 1st time. West Feliciana Parish, Louisiana.

Line of men on the way to the West Feliciana Parish courthouse in St. Francisville, Louisiana to register to vote.

All photographs @2022 Bob Adelman Estate. All rights reserved. Circa 1963.

All who boarded the bus understood this ride would be dangerous as all were aware of the bomb threat on the school bus. Still, they boarded for a ride to the St. Francisville Courthouse, prepared to risk their lives.

West Feliciana Parish Courthouse, St. Francisville, La.

Black men and women sit across the street from the Courthouse while awaiting their opportunity to vote. Standing: Steve Johnson and Raymond Minor. Seated: Handy Berry, Maria Baker and her daughter, Matlee Stella Baker Blackmore.

All photographs @2022 Bob Adelman Estate. All rights reserved. Circa 1963

Man with knife outside the courthouse in St. Francisville, West Feliciana Parish, La.

All photographs @2022 Bob Adelman Estate. All rights reserved. Circa 1963.

After eight years of trying, the Reverend Joe Carter stands with Ronnie Moore and an unidentified C.O.R.E. civil rights worker. He succeeds in registering to vote, then is jeered as he walks down the courthouse steps, St. Francisville, Louisiana. "Joe Carter was the 1st Black man in his parish to register to vote in the twentieth century — this despite the fact that two out of three residents of the parish were black. Once he succeeded in his quest, danger was in the air. I remember someone at the courthouse shouting at me, 'Take his picture, it may be the last one he takes.'"

Ronnie Moore pinning Rev. Carter with registration button, St. Francisville, West Feliciana, La.

Nathaniel Smith, the 2nd Black man to vote departs the courthouse as Ernest Morgan, the 3rd Black man enters. Although others waited patiently to vote, no Black person was allowed to vote until the following day.

Norvelle Hamilton, Raymond Minor, George Johnson, Ronnie Moore, Eddie Baker, prospective voters, and CORE civil rights workers gather to congratulate Carter and hear about his historic breakthrough, West Feliciana Parish, Louisiana. 1963.

Two men looking at burnt cross West Feliciana Parish, LA 1963. The night after Rev. Joseph Carter became the first black person to register in West Feliciana Parish since the 1920s, crosses were burned across East and West Feliciana parishes by the KKK and its sympathizers.

Reverend Carter, expecting a visit from the Klan after he has dared to register to vote, stands guard on his front porch, West Feliciana Parish, Louisiana, 1963. "After Reverend Carter had registered to vote, that night vigilant neighbors scattered in the woods near his farmhouse, which was at the end of a long dirt road, to help him if trouble arrived. 'If they want a fight, we'll fight,' Joe Carter told me. 'If I have to die, I'd rather die for right.' "He told me, 'I value my life more since I became a registered voter. A man is not a first-class citizen, a number one citizen, unless he is a voter.' After Election Day came and went, Reverend Carter added, 'I thanked the Lord that he let me live long enough to vote."

Photo courtesy of Earline Blackmore

Notable

Mrs. Maria Baker

First Woman of Color to Vote in West Feliciana Parish

(October 14, 1897 – June 30, 2004)

Fondly known as “Mama,” Mrs. Maria Turner Baker was from a family of twelve. Born in Mississippi, the Turner family lived in a home centered between the state lines of Louisiana and Mississippi. Married to Eddie “Papa” Jacob Baker, Sr., Mr. and Mrs. Baker raised four children as farmers. As with most farmers, Papa remained in the fields from early morning until late evening. Mrs. Baker, however, who did not work in the field, enjoyed early morning strolls. She enjoyed hand picking cotton from the cotton patches near the side of her home, caring for her family, and preparing home cooked meals. A kind woman who loved animals, Mrs. Baker welcomed a variety of strays into her yard and fed them mush daily (a combination of left-over foods).

Ms. Earline Blackmore, granddaughter of Mrs. Maria Baker, recalls her grandmother’s involvement in the Civil Rights Movement in St. Francisville as if it were yesterday. “Mama attended meetings in Laurel Hill during the early stage of the Civil Rights Movement. Late in the evenings, most often at seven o’clock, the meeting location moved to the Independence community on Hwy 965 (Audubon Park Road). At the end of each meeting, the entire room would lock arms and sing, ‘We Shall Overcome.’”

CORE Volunteers Ronnie Miller and Mimi Feingold were a few of the volunteers from Baton Rouge who learned how People of Color were organizing in Laurel Hill. Both traveled weekly to offer assistance to the community.

In 1963, Earline Blackmore was a Senior in High School. After graduating from Dawson High in 1964, she commuted by bus to attend Southern University. Every Tuesday evening, without fail, after a full day at college, Earline would go directly to the Voters League Hall for a regularly scheduled meeting. From a young age, she and other teens and young adults assisted the community with memorizing the constitution and preparing families on how to vote.

“When I would get out of school, I would go to the Voters League Hall in the evenings to practice test taking and reading the ballot for community members at the Hall. We would sometimes walk from Independence into the town of St. Francisville, marching for the right to vote.” Says Earline.

During the Civil Rights Movement in St Francisville, Klansmen exercised terrorizing tactics to intimidate and threaten People of Color of their human right to vote. Most often tactics used were guns and cross burnings. Any news that traveled by word of mouth, regarding marches or meetings in the parish, the Klan would appear during the night to threaten People of Color.

The Blackmore Family was West Feliciana's first Black family to purchase property on Canefield Road. Earline's parents, Mr. Quinnie Blackmore, and mother, Matlee Stella Baker Blackmore, were the owners. The road was named for the landowner, Mr. Leon Canfield, who operated a store located on Canefield, currently known as Blackmore Road. Many nights Klansmen drove trucks to the dead-end property of the Blackmore family to threaten them with gunfire. Instructed children were to remain on the floor until the gunfire stopped and the yard was no longer burning with a cross.

"We would try to peep to see what they were doing, and the fire would light up the whole yard with burning crosses, and people wearing white sheets," says Earline. "But the funny thing was, once the cross would burn out, Mama would make us go out to get the wood and put it in our fireplace because of the size. They used brand new pine wood, two by four in size, but Mama kept calm. Even though she didn't show fear, I can't imagine she wasn't." Earline continued, "Every morning, we used to do prayer service around the fireplace. And even though we had to endure this trauma, we never missed a day walking to school. But Mama always used to tell me, 'Gal, if you was comin' up when I was comin' up, you woulda been dead.' And I would always reply, Mama, you taught us that we were supposed to stand up for what was right, and that's what I'm going to do."

Mrs. Maria Baker lived with her husband, Papa, until he died at the age of 97. Mrs. Maria Elizabeth "Mama" Turner Baker lived to the ripe age of 107-years old.

AFFIDAVIT Form No. 11

Question Form Selected
Circle one

1	6
2	(7)
3	8
4	9
5	10

St. Francisville, Louisiana Date October 23 1963

I do solemnly swear that I will faithfully and fully abide by the laws of this State and that I am well disposed to the good order and happiness thereof.

Sworn to and subscribed before me this

____ day of ________, 196__.

____
(Deputy Registrar)

Maria Elizabeth Baker
Applicant's Signature

"Applicant shall demonstrate his ability to read and write from dictation by the Registrar of Voters from the Preamble to the Constitution of the United States of America."

PREAMBLE

We, the people of the United States, in order to form a more perfect union, establish justice, insure domestic tranquility, provide for the common defense, promote the general welfare, and secure the blessings of liberty to ourselves and our posterity, do ordain and establish this Constitution for the United States of America. (Article VIII, 1 (c) (7) La. Constitution)

And secure the blessings of liberty to ourselves and our posterity

CITIZENSHIP TEST FOR REGISTRATION

Circle letter indicating your answers to the four numbered questions you have chosen.

1 — a (b) (c) 3 — a (b) (c) 5 — a b (c)
2 — a (b) (c) 4 — a (b) c 6 — (a) (b) c

(La. Constitution, Article VIII, Sec. 1 (d) and LRS 18:31 (2))

(The above qualification test and a registration application form provided for by Act 63 of 1962, (Form LR-1), were received by me from the West Feliciana Parish Registrar of Voters upon my request to register, and I have signed both for acknowledgement and identification with my application to register.)

Date: October 23, 1963

Ward 9 Precinct 1

Maria Elizabeth Baker
Applicant for Registration
Address Rt. 5A Box 857 St. Francisville, La.

The following are copies of the original Registrar of Voters exam taken by Mrs. Maria Baker. Courtesy of Ms. Earline Blackmore.

DO NOT WRITE ON THIS CARD

Form No. 1

Applicant must correctly answer any four of the following six questions so as to evidence an elemental knowledge of the Constitution and Government, an attachment thereto, and a simple understanding of the obligations of citizenship under a republican form of government.

1. The church that we attend is chosen—
   a. by the National Government.
   b. by ourselves.
   c. by the Congress.

2. The President must be at least—
   a. twenty-five years old.
   b. thirty years old.
   c. thirty-five years old.

3. It is important for every voter—
   a. to vote as others tell him to vote.
   b. to vote for the most popular candidates.
   c. to vote for the best qualified candidates.

4. The name of our first President was—
   a. John Adams.
   b. George Washington.
   c. Alexander Hamilton.

5. The Constitution of the United States places the final authority in our Nation in the hands of—
   a. the national courts.
   b. the States.
   c. the people.

6. The President of the Senate gets his office—
   a. by election by the people.
   b. by election by the Senate.
   c. by appointment by the President.

Applicant's answers must be provided on Form No. 11 furnished by the Registrar for permanent records.

This card must be returned to the Registrar

DO NOT WRITE ON THIS CARD

Form No. 2

Applicant must correctly answer any four of the following six questions so as to evidence an elemental knowledge of the Constitution and Government, an attachment thereto, and a simple understanding of the obligations of citizenship under a republican form of government.

1. The Congress cannot regulate commerce—
   a. between States.
   b. with other countries.
   c. within a state.

2. The general plan of a State government is given—
   a. in the Constitution of the United States.
   b. in the laws of the Congress.
   c. in its own State constitution.

3. The name of our first President was—
   a. John Adams.
   b. George Washington.
   c. Alexander Hamilton.

4. The President gets his authority to carry out laws—
   a. from the Declaration of Independence.
   b. from the Constitution.
   c. from the Congress.

5. Our towns and cities have delegated authority which they get from the—
   a. State.
   b. Congress.
   c. President.

6. A citizen who desires to vote on election day must, before that date, go before the election officers and—
   a. register.
   b. pay all of his bills.
   c. have his picture taken.

Applicant's answers must be provided on Form No. 11 furnished by the Registrar for permanent records.

This card must be returned to the Registrar

DO NOT WRITE ON THIS CARD

Form No. 3

Applicant must correctly answer any four of the following six questions so as to evidence an elemental knowledge of the Constitution and Government, an attachment thereto, and a simple understanding of the obligations of citizenship under a republican form of government.

1. The legislative branch of the State government—
   a. makes the laws for the State.
   b. tries cases in the courts.
   c. explains the laws.

2. Limits are placed on the right to vote by the—
   a. National Government.
   b. States.
   c. courts.

3. The powers granted to the National Government in the Constitution are called—
   a. delegated powers.
   b. denied powers.
   c. the final authority.

4. The name of our first President was—
   a. John Adams.
   b. George Washington.
   c. Alexander Hamilton.

5. The Constitution of the United States places the final authority in our Nation in the hands of—
   a. the national courts.
   b. the States.
   c. the people.

6. Each State has as many Presidential electors as it has—
   a. Senators.
   b. Representatives.
   c. Senators and Representatives.

Applicant's answers must be provided on Form No. 11 furnished by the Registrar for permanent records.

This card must be returned to the Registrar

DO NOT WRITE ON THIS CARD

Form No. 4

Applicant must correctly answer any four of the following six questions so as to evidence an elemental knowledge of the Constitution and Government, an attachment thereto, and a simple understanding of the obligations of citizenship under a republican form of government.

1. In case of impeachment of the President, the officer who would preside at the trial is—
   a. the Vice President.
   b. the Speaker of the House of Representatives.
   c. Chief Justice of the United States.

2. Money is coined by—
   a. the States.
   b. the people.
   c. the National Government.

3. Our Constitution has been changed—
   a. by the President.
   b. by the Congress and the people.
   c. by the Supreme Court.

4. Limits are placed on the right to vote by the—
   a. National Government.
   b. States.
   c. courts.

5. The Constitution of the United States places the final authority in our Nation in the hands of—
   a. the national courts.
   b. the States.
   c. the people.

6. The name of our first President was—
   a. John Adams.
   b. George Washington.
   c. Alexander Hamilton.

Applicant's answers must be provided on Form No. 11 furnished by the Registrar for permanent records.

This card must be returned to the Registrar

The following are copies of the original Registrar of Voters exam taken by Mrs. Maria Baker. Courtesy of Ms. Earline Blackmore.

DO NOT WRITE ON THIS CARD Form No. 7

Applicant must correctly answer any four of the following six questions so as to evidence an elemental knowledge of the Constitution and Government, an attachment thereto, and a simple understanding of the obligations of citizenship under a republican form of government.

1. The State governments have the authority to—
   a. admit new States into the Union.
   b. set up local governments within the State.
   c. declare war.

2. The Seventeenth Amendment states that Senators shall be elected by—
   a. the State legislatures.
   b. the people of the States.
   c. the Congress.

3. The Constitution of the United States places the final authority in our Nation in the hands of—
   a. the national courts.
   b. the States.
   c. the people.

4. Presidential candidates are nominated—
   a. by State Legislatures.
   b. by National Conventions.
   c. by the people.

5. The written statement of the things for which a political party stands is called the—
   a. ballot.
   b. platform.
   c. candidate.

6. The name of our first President was—
   a. John Adams.
   b. George Washington.
   c. Alexander Hamilton.

Applicant's answers must be provided on Form No. 11 furnished by the Registrar for permanent records.

This card must be returned to the Registrar

DO NOT WRITE ON THIS CARD Form No. 8

Applicant must correctly answer any four of the following six questions so as to evidence an elemental knowledge of the Constitution and Government, an attachment thereto, and a simple understanding of the obligations of citizenship under a republican form of government.

1. The number of Representatives from each State depends upon—
   a. the voters.
   b. the population.
   c. the electors.

2. The Senators and Congressmen from my State are elected by the—
   a. State legislature.
   b. voters.

3. The name of our first President was—
   a. John Adams.
   b. George Washington.
   c. Alexander Hamilton.

4. The Constitution of the United States places the final authority in our Nation in the hands of—
   a. the national courts.
   b. the States.
   c. the people.

5. United States judges obtain their offices through—
   a. election by the people of their districts.
   b. appointment by the President without the approval of the Senate.
   c. appointment by the President with the advice and consent of the Senate.

6. A tax on the money a person receives in payment for his labor, or earnings from his property is—
   a. an income tax.
   b. a poll tax.
   c. a sales tax.

Applicant's answers must be provided on Form No. 11 furnished by the Registrar for permanent records.

This card must be returned to the Registrar

DO NOT WRITE ON THIS CARD Form No. 5

Applicant must correctly answer any four of the following six questions so as to evidence an elemental knowledge of the Constitution and Government, an attachment thereto, and a simple understanding of the obligations of citizenship under a republican form of government.

1. The legislative branch of the State government—
   a. makes the laws for the State.
   b. tries cases in the courts.
   c. explains the laws.

2. Limits are placed on the right to vote by the—
   a. National Government.
   b. States.
   c. courts.

3. The powers granted to the National Government in the Constitution are called—
   a. delegated powers.
   b. denied powers.
   c. the final authority.

4. The name of our first President was—
   a. John Adams.
   b. George Washington.
   c. Alexander Hamilton.

5. The Constitution of the United States places the final authority in our Nation in the hands of—
   a. the national courts.
   b. the States.
   c. the people.

6. Each State has as many Presidential electors as it has—
   a. Senators.
   b. Representatives.
   c. Senators and Representatives.

Applicant's answers must be provided on Form No. 11 furnished by the Registrar for permanent records.

This card must be returned to the Registrar

DO NOT WRITE ON THIS CARD Form No. 6

Applicant must correctly answer any four of the following six questions so as to evidence an elemental knowledge of the Constitution and Government, an attachment thereto, and a simple understanding of the obligations of citizenship under a republican form of government.

1. In case of impeachment of the President, the officer who would preside at the trial is—
   a. the Vice President.
   b. the Speaker of the House of Representatives.
   c. Chief Justice of the United States.

2. Money is coined by—
   a. the States.
   b. the people.
   c. the National Government.

3. Our Constitution has been changed—
   a. by the President.
   b. by the Congress and the people.
   c. by the Supreme Court.

4. Limits are placed on the right to vote by the—
   a. National Government.
   b. States.
   c. courts.

5. The Constitution of the United States places the final authority in our Nation in the hands of—
   a. the national courts.
   b. the States.
   c. the people.

6. The name of our first President was—
   a. John Adams.
   b. George Washington.
   c. Alexander Hamilton.

Applicant's answers must be provided on Form No. 11 furnished by the Registrar for permanent records.

This card must be returned to the Registrar

The following are copies of the original Registrar of Voters exam taken by Mrs. Maria Baker. Courtesy of Ms. Earline Blackmore.

Photo courtesy of Mr. Joseph McDomick, Jr.

Notable

The Honorable Joseph McDomick, Jr.

Magistrate of St. Helena

Honorable Joseph "Joe" McDomick, Jr. was a 1956 graduate of John S. Dawson High School and a classmate of Dr. Roberta Emery Nelson. He was born on May 1, 1938, in St. Francisville, La., to the late Joseph McDomick, Sr., and Olivia Steward McDomick. Judge McDomick spent his early years in Wakefield, La., along with his sister, Eunice, and two cousins, Willie and Douglas. All four were raised by his maternal grandmother, Elizabeth Steward (b.1882).

Growing up on a farm, Judge McDomick grew up in a house without running water, electricity, or a radio. "Every chance I had to go to school instead of staying home and working on the farm with my uncle, I would. I'd sometimes lie and tell them I had to take a test, so I can't make it today!" he laughs.

Judge McDomick obtained a Bachelor of Science in Agriculture from Southern University A&M College. Upon graduation in 1961, he departed for South America in December to join the Peace Corps as a volunteer. He spent the next two years working as an Agriculture Extension Assistant with the Brazilian government. He returned to the U.S. in 1963.

The Penn Center was the first school for Blacks in the country. Founded in 1862 by Quakers from Pennsylvania 1862, The Penn Center, initially set up on St. Helena Island, South Carolina, was created as an experiment to see if the enslaved could be educated. Eventually, Penn Center became Penn School, which continued to be the only school on the island to educate Black students until 1953.

It was at the Penn Center where Judge McDomick began a thirty-year career as a Field Supervisor. It was December 1962, a time of civil unrest and community organizing. Judge McDomick started writing grant proposals to assist Blacks in the community. Continually working to improve the lives of the underserved, he brought knowledge of federal assistance programs to the forefront. It was his goal to help those who had yet to earn respectable living wages and to shine a spotlight on the inequalities of People of Color. Due to his efforts, the Penn Center received a $145,000 grant to establish the first Head Start program, the first EOC county program, and the Beaufort-Jasper Comprehensive Health program.

In this space, a fire was lit for now civil rights activist Judge McDomick. Refusing to tolerate discrimination in any form, he assisted his community by filing several lawsuits against local restaurants that refused to serve black customers, picketing businesses that would not hire Blacks in supervisory positions, and eventually formed the Welfare Rights Organization. Being raised on a farm, he turned his attention to coordinating a land retention education program upon the realization that Black landowners were being exploited.

During this period, to become a Magistrate, one must have attended an academy to train and pass a civil and criminal law exam before being appointed by the Governor. Finally, in 1980, Judge McDomick was elected and accepted the appointment as Magistrate of St. Helena Island. It was in the courtroom where he continued to work tirelessly on behalf of those who were under-represented.

Judge McDomick wishes to recognize the following: Mr. Anderolf Stevenson, a John S. Dawson High School 4-H leader, and Mrs. Nan Sherman, a case worker of South Carolina who became the first Black Director of Social Services.

Judge Joseph McDomick has been married to Nersene Brown McDomick from Liberty, Mississippi, since 1965. They have three sons: Joseph III, Philander, and Mark DcDomick. Their daughter, the late Monicha Philander wrote the following about her father: *"The improvement of the heart, hands, head, and health of everyone – the 4-H motto? No. This is, seemingly, one man's only goal in life."* They have nine grandchildren and three great-grandchildren. In his spare time, Judge McDomick enjoys gardening and participating in a farmer's cooperative (organized after his retirement in 2006), but you can always find him fishing as he keeps his boat hitched to the back of his truck. His hope for the future is that humanity can learn to live together in peace and harmony.

Photo courtesy of the J. S. Dawson Foundation

Notable

Dr. Leodrey Williams
Agriculture

An employee of the Cooperative Extension Service for fifty of its one hundred years, Dr. Leodry Williams has been the only person to serve as Chancellor of the Southern University Agriculture Research and Extension Center since its inception.

Born in West Feliciana Parish and graduating from John S. Dawson in 1957, Dr. Williams grew up working on his family farm as a way of life. "It was the only income we had. My father was a farmer, and I started plowing and cultivating the field at a very young age. It was work and going to school," says Dr. Williams. After graduating from John S. Dawson High School, Leodrey enrolled at Southern University and received a degree in Vocational Agriculture and a Doctorate degree from Louisiana State University (LSU).

Williams was not formally introduced to agriculture until high school as a member of the New Farmers of America Program. His participation in the program's quiz bowl contest allowed him to visit Southern University and reside in the dormitories while in high school. After graduating, Williams enrolled at Southern University and originally planned to major in bacteriology. "It sounded good, but I didn't know anything about it, so I majored in Vocational Agriculture." He never planned to use his degree to teach in a classroom but wanted to work in Foreign Services. "I wanted to work internationally in developing countries," said Williams. "That was my interest." [18]

However, things did not work out as planned. Dr. Williams took the Peace Corp exam during his senior year and was selected to go to a foreign country. However, he declined the offer to take a class he needed to graduate and asked to be reassigned later.

Just before his graduation, Williams was drafted into the Army. "I didn't get a chance to go to the Peace Corp. After three years and a couple of months in the Army, that was enough Foreign Service for that time. After that, I was ready to go to my professional job," said Williams.

After returning home from the Army, Dr. Williams visited his former Agriculture teacher, Mr. Chapman, in search of work. Mr. Chapman told him the only position he knew of was an assistant county agent in Richland Parish. And based on the history of that parish and circumstances surrounding civil rights demonstrations, he would not recommend that job. Williams replied, "If a person has one bit of human in him, I'll be able to get there and get along with him." [18]

In 1965, after being hired as the assistant county agent for work with Negros in Richland Parish, Dr. Williams began his professional career in Agriculture with Cooperative Extension. Six weeks later, the title was deemed illegal after passing the Civil Rights Act. Although Dr. Williams was assigned that specific title, he also worked with White farmers. "I worked with some (White farmers) who said I was the only person that worked with them. White agents had never worked with them," said Williams.[18] In 1971, Southern University established its extension office and hired Dr. Williams as an Agricultural Specialist and a small staff to recruit and create programs. Dr. Williams held positions at Southern and Louisiana State University during his lengthy career. As a director, he served on several governmental committees. He was appointed Ombudsman of a national task force organized to ensure the "upward mobility of extension." He would become the National Director of this task force and oversaw funding for extension programs at 104 land-grant universities.

In 1890, Congress passed the Second Morrill Act stipulating that People of Color were included in the land-grant university system. The first Morrill Act was signed into law by President Abraham Lincoln in 1862. There is an 1862 land-grant university in every state, including LSU in Louisiana.[18]

In 1995, Dr. Williams returned to Southern as the Cooperative Extension Director. In 2001, he was asked to lead the newly formed Southern University Agricultural Research and Extension Center, the fifth campus of the Southern University System. He planned to work for two and a half years but held the position for fourteen years. As Chancellor, he focused on growing the center as an intricate part of the Southern University System.

Currently, Dr. Leodrey Williams is retired and lives in Louisiana.

Additional awards and Accomplishments:

- Louisiana Living Legend through the Southern University Agricultural Research and Extension Center.
- Certificate of Recognition for fifty years of service in the field of Agriculture by the Baton Rouge Metro Council.
- Proclamation as 'Mayor-President of East Baton Rouge Parish' for the day by former Mayor President Melvin L. "Kip" Holden.

- Appointed the Acting Administrator of the U.S. Department of Agriculture's Extension Service for all U.S. states and territories.
- Served on several national and international committees.
- Consultant in Extension Administration and Education in Sierra Leone and Ethiopia.
- Helped to develop memoranda of understanding with the Republic of South Africa and the Republic of China.
- Honored with the title of Chancellor Emeritus of the Southern University Agriculture Research and Extension Center.

Part V

The Center of St. Francisville and Black Families

DRINK
Coca-Cola
IN BOTTLES
TEEN AGE CAFE
COLORED
ONLY
DRINK
Coca-Cola
IN BOTTLES
BOLL WEEVIL CAFE
For COLORED
ONLY

Highway 61 is a major US highway which passed through the center of St. Francisville. On this highway was a mix of both the homes of People of Color and Black-Owned business. In St. Francisville, the following is a list of previously Black-Owned businesses: Eugene Givens, Buddy Nettles, Alvin Sims Barbershops, Roxie and Sweetie Beauty parlor, the neighborhood Black Baseball Park, Sal Saloon and The Boll Weevil Café (owned by Samuel and Shirley Hardy Price), The Hoffman Fish Market, Max Johnson's Funeral Home, and William Hoffman, Elnora and Silas Hardy, Jr. were additional mentionable business owners as well.

Barber and Beauty Shops

Alvin Sims, Eugene Givens, and Buddy Nettles Barber Shops served as businesses in St. Francisville not only to get hair care service. People of Color could also get a shoeshine, play cards, checkers, and dominoes while conversing about local "grapevine gossip" and community affairs. Roxie and Sweetie's Beauty Parlor stayed packed on Friday and Saturday evenings.

Churches

Churches and Funeral Homes for People of Color all played an essential role in the St. Francisville community. "It takes a village to raise a child" is a well-known proverb. It takes us back to the meaning of the importance of raising children with support from community members. While growing up in St. Francisville, all young people were disciplined by older adults. It wasn't uncommon for young Black children to receive discipline from an "uncle daddy" who disciplined them more than their parents.

St. Francisville had two Baptist churches: St. Andrew Baptist Church, pastored by Rev. David Grimes, and Raspberry Baptist Church, pastored by Rev. Isaiah Mitchell. I was baptized at St. Andrew Baptist Church.

St. Andrew Baptist Church is the 2nd oldest Black Baptist Church in St. Francisville. During my stay at St. Andrew Baptist Church, I was pastored by Rev. David Grimes. The names of the Deacons included were the following: Sam Lee, James Lenard, James Morrison, Ledell Sterling, Nelson Stevens, Woodrow Stevens, Miles Temple, Dave Williams, and John Williams.

Photo courtesy of Tonya Scott Wyandon – 2022

Service on the 2nd Sunday was exceptionally long because it was a Sunday for "testimony." Each member, including the youth, would come before the church to testify their spiritual faith.

Attending St. Andrew Baptist Church was quite a spiritual experience, especially for young adults. On 3rd Sundays, young adults had to participate in church three times. On 3rd Sundays, we attended Sunday School at 9:00 AM, Church Service at 10:30 AM, and Communion service at 6:30 PM. Communion was considered the Lord's Supper at that time. Since supper was an evening meal, then Communion should be in the evening.

Raspberry Baptist Church was organized in 1866. Raspberry Baptist Church is West Feliciana Parish's oldest independent Black Baptist church. Unlike Afton Villa Baptist Church or Sage Hill Baptist Church, it was never affiliated with a plantation. For reasons not documented in the church's history, the structure was rebuilt in 1873, 1890, and again in 1965. In the 1930's and 1940's, Raspberry Baptist Church was closely affiliated with the grade school established for children of color in the late 1880's. The school's principal was John S. Dawson, formally of the Laurel Hill School, who served as Senior Deacon and Sunday School Superintendent in the church.[12]

St. Andrew Baptist Church and Raspberry Baptist Church were Black Baptist churches in downtown St. Francisville. Other Black Churches in West Feliciana Parish include Afton Villa Baptist Church, Cedar Grove Baptist Church, Elm Park Baptist Church, Hickory Grove Baptist Church, Hollywood Baptist Church, Independence Baptist Church, Rosemound Baptist Church, and Sage Hill Baptist Church.

"Independence Baptist Church is the nearest of all listed Black Churches to downtown St. Francisville in that it is approximately 1.5 miles. Independence Baptist Church was chartered in 1887 but did not occupy its present site until 1908. On March 6, 1920, the congregation was formally incorporated with a mission of buying land to erect a new church and a school. Sarah H. Diedritch Lewis Barrow, of Ambrosia and Independence Plantation helped them realize this goal when she donated 1.09 acres, valued at $50, on April 30, 1920. A new structure was constructed, approximately 50 feet east of the original building. Finally, the church was bricked in 1975, and a back section with indoor bathrooms was added."[12]

"The oldest Baptist Church in West Feliciana Parish for People of Color is Afton Villa Baptist Church. This Church originated from a congregation that worshipped together in the woods of Clover Hill Plantation. On February 9, 1871, Susan Barrow, the mistress of Afton Villa Plantation, donated land near her home so the group could build a church. The congregation then split, with half founding Afton Villa Baptist Church in 1873, and the remaining members established Sage Hill Baptist Church shortly thereafter. The original church house was a small, one-room structure. It was replaced in 1890 by a larger building bricked in 1970. The church was rededicated in 1980." [12]

Sage Hill Baptist Church is considered the second oldest Baptist church for People of Color in West Feliciana Parish. "Following Emancipation, Blacks from the Clover Hill Plantation separated into two worship groups. In 1871, one established Afton Villa Baptist Church and, several months later, the other founded Sage Hill Baptist Church. The current church was built in 1980 to replace the original wooden structure."[12]

Rosemound Baptist Church is the third-oldest African American Baptist Church in West Feliciana Parish. Rosemound Baptist Church (also known as Laurel Hill) was built on land once owned by the Argues, a White family.[12] "They ran the nearby general store and post office. The congregation bought the property from Laura E. Argue in 1882. Still, the church's cornerstone states that the church was not formally established until May 27, 1891. It was at this church that educator John S. Dawson began his 58-year career as a teacher. According to his obituary in the St. Francisville Democrat, he taught in the church from January 1890 until around 1895, when a separate schoolhouse, the Laurel Hill School, was erected."[12]

Pilgrim Rest Cemetery, established in 1904, served Black churches, such as Raspberry Baptist Church and St. Andrew Baptist Church, within the town limits of St. Francisville. The cemetery sits on land donated in the early 1900s by a member of the Williams family (proprietors of the Myrtle plantation from the early 1900s). West Feliciana Parish educator John S. Dawson, for whom John S. Dawson High School was named, is buried at Pilgrim Rest Cemetery.

Photo courtesy of Tonya Scott Wyandon – 2022

Funeral Homes

In 1951, Max Johnson, Sr. established the St. Francisville Funeral Home. The business was in his home on the "Hill," located on North Commerce Street in the Highland Community. After completing the State of Louisiana's entire requirement to become a licensee, on January 8, 1952, Max Johnson, Sr. was awarded his Louisiana State Board of Embalmers and Funeral Directors License. "During the second quarter of 1964, financial resources were secured, land was purchased, and a new chapel at 5914 Commerce Street was certified by the Louisiana State Board of Embalmers and Funeral Directors Agency."[12] This allowed Johnson to provide a complete line of funeral services to the citizens of Louisiana. "The facilities were completed and officially opened in October 1964. This structure was the first and only chapel ever built to provide funeral services in West Feliciana Parish."[12]

It has been said that before 1951, according to my uncle William Jackson, funerals for People of Color were conducted by a Black man, Mr. Wiley Morgan. These funerary rituals traditionally consisted of a wake or visitation, church service, and a burial. As West Feliciana Parish had no People of Color embalmers until 1951, services were frequently held within twenty-four-hour of death so that the uninterred body would not begin to decompose.

Funeral rituals traditionally consisted of a wake, church service, and burial. Funerals frequently took place on the weekends so people would not miss work. Deceased People of Color from the West Feliciana Parish community are buried in church graveyards and St. Francisville's historically cemetery for People of Color, Pilgrim's Rest.

The Hardwood Sports Baseball Team

Photo courtesy of Betty Davis Weaver

The Hardwood Sports Baseball Team

St. Francisville had two baseball teams: the St. Francisville Saints (White) and the Hardwood Sports (Black). The St. Francisville Saints baseball games were played in the baseball park in the center of St. Francisville. The star player for the Saints was Charles B. Wilcox, a speedy, right-handed-hitting outfielder who signed with the Hammond Berries of the Class D Evangeline League in 1948.

The Hardwood Sports was owned by a Black man, Mr. George Miller, and his players included the following: Dale Boxstell, Dan Buster, Ernest Davis (catcher), Robert Jackson, "Jeff" Jefferson (player and acting manager), Frank Pickens (pitcher), Robert Knighten, Liker Lloyd, Ike Snowden, and Edward Whitaker. Other players include (first name only): Bogan, Johnny, Luke, Sunny, and others.

The Hardwood Sports games were held in a baseball park in Hardwood, La. The games drew crowds from as far as New Orleans. After the games, there were lively activities with food, dancing in the streets, and socializing at Club 61 in Hardwood. Music was by artists such as Chuck Berry, John Lee Hooker, Big Joe Turner, Slim Harpo, Lighting Slim. Jimmy Reed, Big Maybelle, T-Bone Walker, and notable local famed blues musician Lil Jimmy Reed.

Photo Courtesy of Betty Davis Weaver

Hardwood Sports Owner, Mr. George Mellon (seated bottom left) with brothers.

George Miller was born in 1892 in Gibson, Mississippi. Fondly known as “Big Daddy” by his greatgrandchildren, George Miller was a quiet, soft-spoken man who enjoyed playing dominos and smoking cigars. In 1948, he and his wife, Georgia Felder Mellon (born in Catawba, Mississippi), relocated to Louisiana. Together they raised one daughter, Willie “Dear” Mae Pickins (the daughter of Georgia Mellon). Pickins. Their daughter, “Dear” became the first in her family to attend High School. She became a Beautician upon graduation and married Herman Davis (a member of Hardwood Sports). They had one daughter, Betty “Mommie” Davis Weaver, who lives in Baton Rouge, La.

George Miller’s responsibilities as owner of Hardwood Sports included management, team representation, travel arrangements, seeking sponsorship, and other financial obligations. Although most revenue came from the games played, members of The Hardwood Sports worked for a living. According to Roderick Hutchinson, former Louisiana Sugar Cane League player and now coach (California), “Players could receive money from spectator side bets. An occasional offering of money slid into a player’s hand, betting by purchasing beer or food was also standard in the South. Even the concession stand proceeds were given to the home team.”

Most games were held in St. Francisville, New Roads, and Baton Rouge, to name a few. During this period, members of The Hardwood Sports included several Cuban baseball players who migrated to the South and played with the team while seeking citizenship during the 1950s.

Kings Lumber Company, located in West Feliciana Parish, operated a boarding house for single, unmarried Black men called Kings Lumber Boarding house. The Boarding house was located next to the woods where the men worked as loggers and mill workers. Both George Miller and his wife, Georgia, worked at the Kings Lumber boarding house as supervisors of the cooks and the cleaning crew. One notable cook in particular was Mrs. Stella Reid. In addition, a public café was located across the street from Club 61 where a pool hall and bar were managed by Mrs. Georgia Miller and identical twin sister, Mrs. Georgia Ann Swift, seven days a week.

Photo courtesy of Betty Davis Weaver

From left to right: Georgia Mellon and twin sister, Georgia Ann Swift.

Photo courtesy of Betty Davis Weaver

Standing from left to right: Georgia Mellon, an unidentified family friend, and Georgia Ann Swift. Bottom left to right: Unidentified family friend and Dorothy (Dot) Nell Mellon Brown.

Photo Courtesy of Betty Davis Weaver

Seventh from left: Willie "Dear" Mae Mellon poses with a group of young women during a school social. Kentwood High Boarding School – Kentwood, La.

Boy Scouts (Colored)

Willard Anderson, Sr. was born in St. Francisville, La near Bayou Sara. Married to Beatrice Barrow Anderson, they had five sons: Willard Jr., Hillard (deceased), Emmett, Harry "HB" Baker (deceased), and Herbert Anderson.

Photo courtesy of Dyvar Anderson

Beatrice, Willard Sr., grandson Herbert Jr. Herbert Sr., grandson Charles, and granddaughter, Dyvar.

During the early 1950s, young Black boys could participate as Boy Scouts in St. Francisville, thanks to Troupe Master Willard Anderson, Sr. Their activities included picnics and learning how to swim at Thompson Creek (the only location for People of Color to swim).

"My dad, Herbert, was born on Christmas day," says Dr. Ajile A. Rahman. "My grandma mentioned by the time she was twenty-three, she'd finished having all her children. Due to lack of medical care, when my father was born, my grandfather went out into the community to get help with birthing. When he discovered his wife was leaving this world, he went into the kitchen to make black coffee, slapped my grandmother's face a few times, and commanded her to wake up. Thankfully, she came around." The catalyst which started Willard Anderson on the road to religious and community activism in the community came through a chance encounter with a life-and-death situation. "When my father was young, my grandfather would take him everywhere. Then, one day, they went out to fish, and a terrible storm came up. My grandfather had to get out of the boat and walk to safety, and the water was so deep it traveled up to his waist. And so, my grandfather put Herbert, my dad, on his shoulders and prayed to God if He saved the two of them, he would dedicate his life to serving God."

Fondly known in the community as "Mr. Big Willard," Willard Anderson was a deacon, and a trustee in the church. He would often pick kids up from the county side in his 1930 Chevy to attend Sunday School. During this time, the school Superintendent was Mr. David Chase, and Mrs. Anderson acted as the Sunday School teacher. During this time, the community was alive with acts of service. Mr. Hoffman often drove his bus to provide transportation for children and donated supplies from his store for cooking. "Saturday night fish fries were important because this was how money was raised for the church," says Dr. Rahman. "The men caught the fish, and the women prepared dinners for the men to take across the street to sell to the patrons at the bar. The amount of work my grandfather dedicated to his community could not have been done without the help of my grandmother."

Photo courtesy of Dyvar Anderson

Anderson's grandchildren: H.B. (named after his deceased uncle), Herbert Jr., Dyvar, wife Beatrice, Charles, and Willard Anderson, Sr.

Dyvar Anderson Wright (daughter to Emmett) serves on several boards in West Feliciana Parish. One organization, the Old Benevolent Society Restoration Committee, is near to her heart. It is at the Old Benevolent Society, which her grandparents, uncles, and many members of the Black community frequently visited when she was a child. Membership included dues that were managed as a form of security for a 'decent' burial. Dyvar has donated several benevolent society artifacts belonging to her family, currently on display at the West Feliciana Historical Society and Museum. "The mission to restore the Benevolent Society is to create the first African-American History Museum that will save our history as well as participate in our future endeavors," says Wright.

To raise funds to restore an important part of our history, Wright is the producer for two major fundraisers in the parish for this restoration project. Sounds of the Season is a concert held during Christmas in the Country featuring a notable Southern University alumni and additional local African American talent. The 1st Annual 2023 Tell the Story Cultural Festival will be held every February in

Parker Park, St. Francisville. This festival will showcase cultural food, handmade arts and crafts, while celebrating the story of family history and culture. Wright's father, Emmett Anderson attended Southern University, left for WWII, and departed from the south permanently to receive his Bachelor of Architecture at Howard University. He lived in Washington DC and is buried there.

Willard Anderson, Sr's son, Herbert Anderson, graduated with honors from Southern University with a degree in Elementary Education in 1955. He later earned a master's degree and a specialist degree in Education. Herbert Anderson, who was commissioned as a Second Lieutenant in the United States Army, was instrumental in the desegregation of LSU in 1955 following Brown vs the Board of Education Supreme Court decision. After being wounded by a sniper at LSU, Herbert Anderson became a member of the Civil Rights Commission, the NAACP, the Boy Scouts, and other Civic Organizations. Mr. Anderson spent time in St. Tammany Parish as a teacher and later as a principal at Alton Junior High School in Slidell. He provided active leadership in the peaceful desegregation of St. Tammany Parish Public Schools in the 1960s. While his time in St. Tammy parish was brief, Herbert Anderson's impact will be felt for generations in the future.

A Prince Hall Mason man, Mr. Anderson would often tell his sons, "If you're a man, you have to pay your way." Willard Anderson paved his way by dedicating his life to service and religious activism. He was buried in St. Francisville in 1967.

Photo courtesy of Dyvar Anderson Dyvar and her grandfather, Willard Anderson

Part VI

Activities for People of Color in St. Francisville, Louisiana

Happy Llandiers

A community service organization, The Happy Llandiers originated in 1955 by a group of Black female teachers. Their focus was to help children within the community. Their mission: To aid young mothers and children in need and student enrichment programs. Some of the programs sponsored by The Happy Llandiers include Teen Outreach (tutoring), summer camps, workshops and more.

The Happy Llandiers began when ten female teachers in West Feliciana Parish unified. They purchased shoes, clothing, and school supplies for children whose families could not afford them. The original Happy Llandiers Civic Club included the following members: Ms. Hilda Anderson, Mrs. Georgia N. Cavalier, Mrs. B. Davidson, Mrs. Alice Dawson, Ms. Brunetta Dawson, Mrs. S. Green, Mrs. Emma S. Harrison, Mrs. Gertrude Romsey, Ms. Velma Smith, and Mrs. M. C. Woods.

Photo courtesy of The Happy Llandiers, St. Francisville, La.

Seated from left to right: Mrs. A.P. Dawson, Ms. Velma Smith,
Mrs. G.N. Cavalier, Ms. Brunetta M. Dawson
Standing from left to right: Mrs. B. Davidson, Mrs. M.C. Woods, Mrs. E.S. Harrison, Mrs. G. Romsey, Ms. H. Anderson, and Mrs. S. Green.

An Educational Visionist

President Emeritus of Happi Llandiers honored

Mrs. Georgia Cavalier, President Emeritus of the Happi Llandiers, was honored June 29

Mrs. Georgia Cavalier

at the St. Luke Baptist Church in the Solitude Community.

Georgia and Alice Pearl Dawson called a group of teachers together to formulate a plan to get the black children of West Feliciana Parish to come to school daily and to get the best education possible. They made a survey and found that most of theses students had to work to survive and lacked clothing and food to come to school.

The Happi Llandiers Club was organized in 1955. The group solicited donations of food, money and clothes. They also trained these students to participate in activities to raise funds to support the idea.

It was a great success and is still working. The children were given what they needed to come to school.

They learned many things through activities.The parents, teachers, and school officials, and merchants all helped.

Georgia was elected president for the first two years. Hilda Anderson and May Courtney Woods served the next two years. Georgia was reelected.

She served 40 years.

With a master's degree in elementary education, Cavalier taught at many different schools including Greenwood Church School, and Rosenwald Elementary. When Rosenwald Elementary consolidated with Dawson, she taught there.

Soon the Bains Junior High was built and she taught there. The move brought many changes. The first change was to departmentalize the classes, to give teacher more time to prepare in the field. Two music teachers were added.

She brought the United Way President to meet with the Police Jury so that United Way could be accepted in the parish in 1985.

The plan worked, and Happi-Llandiers received an allotment from United Way.

In 1987, Happi Llandiers was accepted as an agent of the United Way.

Georgia was married to the late Daniel Cavalier and has two children, Daniel Cavalier, Jr., and Deanne Annette Cavalier Henagan.

Reprint with permission – Happi Llandiers, St. Francisville, La.

This all-female, non-profit organization formed in 1955 is stronger today than ever. To date, every school year, The Happy Llandiers, Inc., spend months soliciting and collecting donations from area businesses. These donations are used for supplies for distribution to students from kindergarten through the twelfth grade.

Photo courtesy of the J. S. Dawson Foundation

Order of The Eastern Star

St. Francisville's all-female chapter of the "Order of the Eastern Star" is based on some teaching from the Bible but is open to all religious beliefs. Members of the order of Eastern Star are aged eighteen and older. Originally, a woman would have to be the daughter, widow, wife, sister, or mother of a Mason. Currently, members of the St. Francisville "Order of Eastern Star" include Beatrice Anderson, Emma Anderson, Sarah Anderson, Alma Booker, Elme Canty, Georgia Cavalier, Fredonia Dawson, Beatrice Duncan, Viola Duncan, Barbara Forman, Carrie Forman, Elnora Givens, Ellen Hardy, Elnora Hardy, Lizzie Harris, Audrey Howard, Katie Mae Johnson, Barbara Lacy, Elizabeth Lee, Lee Alice McQuirter, Shirley Price, Alberta Richardson, Doretha Robinson, Brunetta Smith, Alme Spruel, Beatrice Stevens, Maria Stevens, Corine Sterling, Margaret Sterling, Annette White, and Camilla White.

Photo courtesy of "Tell the Story", St. Francisville, La.

Photo courtesy of "Tell the Story," St. Francisville, La.

The Benevolent Society

The St. Francisville Old Benevolent Society building, built in 1883, played a significant role in the lives of People of Color in West Feliciana Parish as the oldest burial insurance lodge. The Benevolent Society filled an urgent need for medical care and burials. Over time, the Benevolent Society provided union and fellowship among People of Color. During the 19th and 20th centuries, nearly every church in West Feliciana Parish had a benevolent society. It was out of the dire needs for People of Color for matters of importance such as sitting with the sick, feeding the hungry, funding medical care, and covering the cost of a decent funeral.

CONSTITUTION

AND BY-LAWS

OF THE

Grand Benevolent Society

Organized June 1, 1919.

FAITH :: HOPE :: CHARITY

We join our hands and hearts together in love and with one another in the name of the Lord to form this association.

The Old Benevolent Society building, located on Ferdinand Street, was built in 1883. Benevolent societies played an important role in black communities following the Civil War. Originally formed to cover the expenses of medical care and burial, they also provided union and fellowship, especially to the sick and weak. Use of this building ceased in December 2016 due to needed repairs to the foundation and exterior. Order of the Eastern Star members have begun working with the West Feliciana Historical Society to initiate efforts to preserve and restore the Old Benevolent Society building.

CONSTITUTION.

PREAMBLE.

We, a body of colored people of the Weyanoke community and a radius of three miles, more or less, from this, the Grand Benevolent Society Hall, in the parish of West Feliciana, feeling that God, in His wise providence, based the universe on the principles of union and that we should try to imitate Him in all that we do, do organize ourselves into a body known as the Grand Benevolent Society.

Article 1. The name and title of this association shall be called the Grand Benevolent Society. There shall be a president, vice-president, secretary, assistant secretary, treasurer, chaplain, six stewards, twelve stewardesses, three marshals and a speaker of the house.

Article 2. It shall be the duty of the president to preside over all meetings of the society with full power. Any law can be changed by the action of two-thirds of the members of this body.

Photo courtesy of "Tell the Story," St. Francisville, La.

The Masonic Lodge

Masonic Lodge (J.S. McGehee Lodge no. 54), built in 1955, replaced the lodge's original meeting place in the Laurel Hill School. During the fall of 1963, the building housed weekly voter registration clinics organized by local activists and members of CORE (Congress of Racial Equality). On October 17, 1963, it was from this building that local ministers, Reverend Carter and Reverend Davis, along with other members of the community, made their historic trip to St. Francisville to register to vote.

The symbols on the building's facade represent, on the right, the Freemasonry fraternal organization and, on the left, the Order of the Eastern Star, the oldest sorority-based Black women's organization in America.[13] During this period, the epicenters of entertainment for People of Color in West Feliciana Parish were St. Francisville, Hardwood, and Solitude. Since Afton Villa and John Dawson High School were the only schools for People of Color, we got to know and interacted with everyone in the parish. The John S. Dawson High School site was located approximately three and a half miles northwest of St. Francisville. Hardwood is located halfway between John S. Dawson High School site and St. Francisville.

Many of us attended baseball games, basketball games, football games, and other functions at Southern University. Also, many of the males traveled across the Mississippi River to the town of New Roads for functions and dated girls we met at athletic activities and record hops.

The town of New Roads is located in Pointe Coupee Parish, directly across the Mississippi River from St. Francisville. We traveled from St. Francisville to New Roads by way of a ferry. We had to coordinate our visits since the ferry stopped running at 10 PM. If we missed the last ferry, we had to travel to Baton Rouge to get home. The "Old Ferry Landing" was the boarding location of the New Roads/St. Francisville Ferry.

In New Roads, it was from these functions that my classmate Willie B. Scott fell in love with Joyce Louis. Both Willie, from St. Francisville, and Joyce, from New Roads attended and graduated from Southern University with a Master of Education. They married and had three children, James Terrald Scott, (deceased), Tonya Scott Wyandon, and Tracey Scott Dkyes.

During those days, music was provided by radio station WXOK-AM with Ray "Diggy Doo" Meaders. WXOK served the Black community since February 3, 1953, with a mixture of R&B, Blues, Jazz, and Gospel until 2000, when it went full-time with Gospel. On behalf of WXOK, "Diggy Doo" provided Friday night record hops throughout the parish. Diggy Doo would sign on and off by saying, "Like a snake in the lake, too slim to swim; like a roach on the porch, too smooth to move; nobody do it like the Diggy do it!" In 1954, with the help of Diggy Doo, Lightin' Slim emerged on the blues scene. On May 30, 1957, Buddy Guy recorded a demo for WXOK, and it was D.J. "Diggie Doo" who sent a copy to Ace Records in Jackson, Mississippi. "Like his idol B.B. King, Buddy Guy rose to the top of the blues world from humble beginnings as a sharecropper's son. His father, Sam Guy bought Buddy his first guitar from another field hand, Henry 'Coot' Smith. 'Coot' showed Buddy how to play John Lee Hooker's 'Boogie Chillen', which was already the favorite record in the Guy household."[2]

Further inspired locally by Lightin' Slim, Buddy began playing in Baton Rouge, La., with 'Big Poppa Tilley and Raful Neal. The flamboyance of Eddie 'Guitar Slim' Jones left a lasting impression. Guy said, "I wanted to play like B. B. but act like Guitar Slim."[2]

At night, we listened to Randy's Record Shop from Nashville, Tennessee, with John Richbourg. "He was a White disc jockey who attained fame in the 1950s and 1960s for playing rhythm and blues music on Nashville station WLAC. He was also a notable record producer and artist manager."[3] Announcers who showcased popular Black music in nightly programs from the late 1940s to the early 1970s were: Gene Nobles, Bill "Hoss Man" Allen, Herman Grizzard, and Rufus (Walking the Dog) Thomas. "Later, rock music disc jockeys, such as Alan Freed and Wolfman Jack, mimicked Richbourg's practice of using speech that simulated the street language of Blacks of the mid-twentieth century."[3]

"Richbourg's highly stylized approach to the on-air presentation of both music and advertising earned him popularity with the public. Yet, his style created confusion about what his racial identity was." Richbourg and, his fellow disc jockey Allen, used speech patterns that often belonged to many People of Color. So, this led to many listeners thinking that both announcers were Black. The disc jockeys used the mystery to their advantage to gain a higher commercial status until the mid-1960s. During the mid-1960s, the public learned that they were White, and they lost their advantage.[3]

During this time, Gospel Music consisted of songs by Inez Andrews, Alex Bradford, Five Blind Boys, Sam Cooke and the Soul Stirrers, Thomas A. Dorsey, Highway Q.C.'s, Dixie Hummingbirds, Brother Joe May, Mahalia Jackson, Mighty Clouds of Joy, The Nightingales, Staple Singers, Swan Silverstone's, Pilgrim Travelers, Albertina Walker, Clara Ward, and others.

Popular Blues music at that time was by the following groups: Brook Benton, Chuck Berry, Bobby Blue Bland, Charles Brown, Solomon Burke, Ray Charles, Fats Domino, Elmore James, Albert King, B.B. King, John Lee Hooker, Lighting Hopkin, Junior Parker, Big Maybelle, Lloyd Price, Jimmy Reed, Little Richard, Bobby Rush, Johnny Taylor, Big Mama Thornton, Rufus Thomas, Big Joe Turner, T-Bone Walker, Muddy Waters, and others.

Photo by permission of Leon "Lil Jimmy Reed" Atkins

Notable

Leon "Lil Jimmy Reed" Atkins
Blues Musician

World-renowned Leon Atkins (Leon’s birth father’s last name) is a native of Hardwood, Louisiana, in West Feliciana Parish. He is the eldest of four brothers and one sister. Leon learned the struggles and discrimination of growing up poor and Black in the deep south at an early age. He was a 1957 graduate of Dawson High School, and his early childhood years were spent in school at a church in Hardwood.

His stepfather, Tom Smith, was the owner of Tom’s Shoe Shop. As Leon grew into his early teenage years, this was where he spent most of his after-school days repairing and shining shoes alongside his mother, Velma Johnson Smith. Leon recalls the era of having to repair shoes out of necessity as it was difficult to purchase new shoes. Leon fondly recalls other Black-owned businesses such as Monday’s Café and Stella Reid Café.

Always with a harmonica in his pocket and favoring music over manual labor, his life changed the day his stepfather secured an income tax return. Tom Smith granted Leon’s sister a doll, his three brothers’ BB guns and balls to play with and granted Leon’s wish for an electric guitar. His dream of someday becoming a famous guitar player was soon to come to fruition.

Five days after receiving his first guitar on a Monday, Leon Atkins boldly stepped onto the stage of Club 61 to perform his first act. It was a Saturday night, and he was only sixteen years old. Nevertheless, he fondly recalls his ability to listen to music during his formative years as “a gift from God.”

Club 61 was located across the street from where Leon Atkins lived. Many nights he lay on his back in bed while listening to many Blues performers such as Muddy Waters and Slim Harpo, to name a few. But for Leon, one performer influenced his style the most; it was the legendary Blues performer Jimmy Reed. His lucky break came the night his idol, Jimmy Reed performed in Baton Rouge, La.

Word around town had spread about Lil Jimmy Reed’s ability to imitate Jimmy Reed. Then, on the night Jimmy Reed was scheduled to perform, the club disc jockey realized he was too intoxicated. Knowing Leon was present, they “eased Jimmy Reed out the back door and brought him through the front door.” That was the night that 18-year-old Leon Atkins became Lil Jimmy Reed. “People never knew the difference,” he said.

With the realization of more stability, Leon decided to join the U.S. Army in 1972 for a twenty-year career. Although he attempted to join the military band, he was unable to perform due to mandatory regulations of being able to read music. Upon retiring from his military duties, it was then he would be free to continue to follow through with his childhood dream of being a full-time blues entertainer as Lil Jimmy Reed.

With his harmonica and guitar in tow, Lil Jimmy Reed has played worldwide, with the exception of China and Japan. Most of his tours are overseas, and he is currently touring. When home in Alabama, Reed gives back to his local community by performing a one-hour set at a total of twelve nursing homes. “Most residents don’t leave their room until they know I’m coming,” he says. “They rise up from their chairs to walk and dance when I come.”

He has been honored with the Key to the City of St. Francisville and has had several appearances at the High School as a special guest. When close to home, he also performs at the annual Baton Rouge BluesFest. Looking back, Lil Jimmy Reed only has one regret. Although he often played with the Jimmy Reed band, he never had the opportunity to meet his idol, Jimmy Reed.

Performers he has both opened and performed with include: the legendary B.B. King, Bobby Blue Bland, Ike Turner, Little Milton, Marvin Cease, Clarence Carter, and Tabby Thomas, to name a few. Lil Jimmy Reed is married to Imogene McKnight Atkins. They have seven daughters, one son, thirty-seven grandchildren, and twenty-four great-grandchildren.

Photo courtesy of Thomas Dawson

Notable

Thomas Dawson

Musician / Producer / Composer

An accomplished musician, Thomas Dawson has always been on the cutting edge of ingenuity. His experience as a musician, combined with his knowledge of computer technology, has made Thomas one of the most sought-after studio engineers in the business.

The grandson of John S. Dawson, Sr., the son of Thomas Dawson, Sr., and Alice Roberts Dawson, Thomas Dawson was born in St. Francisville and graduated from West Feliciana High School in 1976.

His recollection of wanting to play instruments was early when most children had other interests. In the fourth grade, the first instrument Thomas played was the drum in the Bains Elementary Band and from middle to high school, he played the trumpet. In addition to school and social performances, Thomas was also an active pianist and organist in several local churches.

Thomas attended Southern University A&M College on a band scholarship under the watchful eye of the late, legendary Issac (Doc) Greggs for five years. There he played the trumpet for three years while working as a student undergraduate assistant band director. Then, in 1978, his gift of music afforded an unexpected opportunity when Dr. Greggs offered Thomas a spot to play guitar with the Ambassadors of Music for the State of Louisiana. This elite sextuplet allowed Thomas Dawson to play independently outside of Southern University. As a side note, prior to Dr. Issac Greggs position of Ambassador of Music, this title was preceded by world-renowned New Orleans native Louis Armstrong.

After college, Thomas worked as a Record Producer for Baton Rouge's first black-owned Recording Studio, "Royal Shield." Later Thomas relocated to Nashville, Tennessee to become part owner of another recording studio while acting as producer, recording engineer, and musician.

In 1988, Thomas and his wife, Roslyn Anderson Dawson (formerly of Baton Rouge), relocated to Los Angeles. It was in LA where Thomas continued his presence on the music scene. One year later, in 1989, Thomas was hired by the world-renowned Commodores as a keyboard/pianist. Thomas has been performing, co-writing, co-producing, and touring with the group for thirty-three years as Music Director.

In addition, Thomas Dawson and Board-Certified Dr. Bambi Nickelberry are the Los Angeles-based Heart for Harmonic Health and Energy co-founders. Dr. Nickelberry, who specializes in blending Western and Eastern medicine and other modalities, partners with Dawson, who offers vibroacoustic (musical frequencies) to facilitate therapeutic healing.

Bio for Notable Thomas Dawson

- Music Director, Co-Producer, and keyboardist for the legendary and world-renowned Commodores.
- Worked with other musical greats, including Beyonce and J Lo.
- A & R representative for Dream Gospel Records.
- Owner and operator of Mountain Nest Recording and Mastering Studios in Colorado Springs. They are currently in production on several soon-to-be-released C.D.s and films.
- Recipient of a BET Jazz Discovery award.
- Gold Album (songwriter) for Changing Faces – All Day, All Night.
- Part Owner of Mackie Manns Film Company, Atlanta, Ga.
- Partner of Production Point in Colorado Springs, Colorado.
- Composer and producer of music for films
- 2021 Dove Award Nominee for Inspirational Film of the Year, "My Brother's Keeper.

Part VII

The West Feliciana Historical Society Cancels the Audubon Pilgrimage

The West Feliciana Historical Society was founded in 1969 to foster an awareness of local history in the belief that a communal sense of continuity and a common past can give hope for the future and help for the present. The certainty that a known past and a sense of place open the doors of the mind has guided its endeavors.[7]

Local St. Francisville Author Anne Butler and Artist Darrell Chitty released their new book "The Soul of St. Francisville," published in 2020. This full-color hardback book features incredible images and portraiture by Chitty, combined with a fond look at the area's small-town charm by Butler, a longtime Louisiana resident. According to a news release, the book culminates several years of work and half a century of research. In its 160 pages, "The Soul of St. Francisville" celebrates the small-town charm and natural beauty of the area, with incredible portraits and photographs complemented by text brimming with little-known historical facts about iconic places and faces.

Butler has roots in the St. Francisville area going back to the late 1700s and is passionate about preserving the state's fragile cultural landscapes, especially its history. Chitty lives in the Shreveport area but has visited the parish for many years, bringing other artists from around the world for workshops.

In June of 2020, the West Feliciana Historical Society canceled its annual Audubon Pilgrimage after a petition criticized the festival for failing to recognize the history of the Black community. "If it is truly going to be an exploration of the past, we have to see all sides of history at that time."[8]

Hannah Leming, who started the petition, said she enjoyed going to the festival during her childhood but has realized the event is not inclusive to members of the Black community.[8]

"I grew up going to the Audubon Pilgrimage wearing dresses and dancing the Maypole. It was an enjoyable part of my childhood. But time, reflection, listening, and learning from the Black community has made me realize that the Pilgrimage is part of the system of oppression. For example, when students are brought to rural homesteads for field trips, White and Black students are either given or encouraged to buy wooden paddles engraved with their names and whips. Both objects were used to torture enslaved people, without explanation." She continues, "I remember going to Oakley Plantation on a field trip and the whole plantation life being glorified. The full history of oppression was never told to my Black classmates or me. We didn't see the slave quarters, and they were never mentioned as being a part of this 'educational' field trip." So Leming states in the petition. Hannah Leming's petition called for either the Audubon Pilgrimage to be canceled in solidarity with the Black Lives Matter movement or be changed to illuminate BOTH sides of history. This resulted in The West Feliciana Historical Society issuing the statement that it would permanently cancel the Audubon Pilgrimage."[8]

The officials with the West Feliciana Historical Society state, "After listening to our community stakeholders and understanding the world and community in which we live, the West Feliciana Historical Society has canceled the Annual Audubon Pilgrimage going forward. We will focus our efforts on providing a complete and accurate history of our parish in a meaningful way that is relevant today and, in the future."[8]

This move is part of a broader nationwide movement following the killing of several Black men and women. The following are a few mainstream names that drew worldwide media attention: George Floyd in Minneapolis, Minnesota; Ahmaud Arbery in Georgia; and Breonna Taylor in Louisville, Kentucky. Their deaths have spurred nationwide and global reckoning regarding police practices and racial injustice, leading to calls for policy changes. Recent protests in some U.S. and European cities have included calls to remove public statues memorializing Confederate and colonial figures. Since 2019 many statues have been toppled by protestors.

Unlike efforts to scrub away the figures, some community members in St. Francisville say they want to see festivals like the Audubon Pilgrimage include Black history.

"We need to be able to tell our story," said Amanda Moorer, a former St. Francisville middle school teacher who supported the petition. "There's a lot to gain from knowing where you come from and where you're trying to move forward to. St. Francisville is a great place, a great community. Still, certain things need to change," she said. "We can do better."

Photo courtesy of Mrs. Yava Scott

Notable

Milton L. Scott

CEO

(November 21, 1956 – December 8, 2019)

The first African American Partner at Arthur Anderson, Houston, Tx and highest ranking African American at a Houston-based Fortune 500 Company, Houston, Texas, the late Milton L. Scott was born in November of 1956. With a passion for excellence, even as a child, he was never content with the status quo. Milton's early days working on the family farm helped shape his views and values of working smarter, not harder. Raised in St. Francisville, La, he was valedictorian of his senior class and quarterback for the high school varsity football team.

A defining moment for Milton came during the summer of his Jr. year in college. Milton's father, Bennett, inquired about a summer job with a local plant manager for his son. For years, his father was also aware that the plant only hired White students for the summer program. Bennett, who was just as outspoken, inquired about the process, and the manager agreed to a meeting. Both father and son attended the interview as, in Milton's mind, he already had the job. Impressed, the plant manager decided to try Bennett's son. But to his surprise, Milton asked, "excuse me, but you still haven't told me what I'll be doing." Once Milton was informed that his work included manual labor, he stood up from his chair, held both hands up to the manager, and said, "look, I'm sorry, but these hands don't fit a shovel. My hands are for a computer." Milton thanked the plant manager and walked out the door with his father following behind him. After a quiet walk to the car, Bennett looked at his son and told him what was said in the White man's office was very clear. He told Milton, "I hope you can stand up to your reputation, son." Milton's response was, "yes, sir. No disrespect, Dad, but I'm glad they understand that. I'm going to find a job where *I'm* in the position of authority." Milton's promise not only to his dad, but to himself never wavered.

Milton graduated from Southern University A&M College, earning a Bachelor of Science in Accounting in three years, and becoming a Certified Public Accountant licensed in Texas for Arthur Anderson, LLP. In 1990, he was admitted to the partnership at Arthur Anderson.

After twenty-two years with Arthur Anderson, in 1999, Milton joined Dynegy as Executive Vice President and Chief Administrative Officer. At that time, he was the highest-ranking African American at a Houston-based Fortune 500 Company. At Dynegy, he devised and implemented a diversity and inclusion strategy, which led to the Board of Directors' transformation to include minorities and women for years to come. He left Dynegy in 2002 to become an entrepreneur as Co-Founder, Managing Director, and CFO of Complete Energy Holdings, LLC., a company that owns and operates power generation assets in the United States. Milton's background in financial structuring was showcased with Complete Energy's second acquisition of La Paloma Generating Facility near Bakersfield, Ca. for $580 million. This move, in turn, was hailed by Project Finance International as "The Power Deal of the Year" in 2005.

In 2007, Milton founded the Tagos Group, LLC, where he served as founder, Chairman, and CEO until his passing in 2019 due to pancreatic cancer.

"Because of my dad, for the rest of my life, whenever I doubt myself, feel a little less than, fail, or make a mistake, I just get back up; I push on," says his daughter, Kirsten. "Not because I am uniquely strong or resilient or talented or virtuous, it is because my father was."

Milton's son, Kameron Scott, adds, "The biggest thing my dad instilled in me was discipline. You see, in his house, there was no 'deserve', the word was 'earned'. If you didn't work for it, then you didn't deserve to get it, and you were not allowed to quit. He encouraged me to always see it through, no matter how hard it gets."

Milton and his wife, Yava Williams Scott (attorney), were married for thirty-seven years. Their two children, Kirsten Scott Bell, lives in Austin, Tx, with her husband, Chris Bell, and daughter, Eloise. Kirsten is a Content Policy Manager at Facebook (Meta). Milton's son, Kameron, also lives in Austin, Tx, and is a Security Specialist for IBM-Global.

Bio for Notable Milton L. Scott:

Professional and Community Boards

- Chairman of the Board, Sterling Construction Company (Nasdaq-Strl)
- Lead Director of W.H. Energy Services, Inc. (formerly NYSE)
- Advisory Board – The CapStreet Group (A private equity firm based in Houston)
- Board of Visitors, M.D. Anderson Cancer Center
- Advisory Council, McCombs School of Business – The University of Texas at Austin
- The Museum of Fine Arts, Houston - Executive Committee and Chairman of the Finance Committee
- Memorial Hermann Healthcare System
- Chairman of the Texas Business Hall of Fame Foundation

- Chairman of the Greater Houston Convention and Visitors Bureau
- Chairman of the University of Texas-Austin McCombs School of Business Foundation

Awards

- The Top 100 African Americans in Business by Savoy Magazine
- The Texas Legislative Caucus Outstanding Texan Award
- The National Achievement Award/ National Association of Black Accountants, Inc.
- The Distinguished Alumni Award from Southern University A&M College
- Southeast YMCA Achievement Award
- The Young CPA of the Year from the Texas Society of Certified Public Accountants
- Texas Society of Certified Public Accountants-Legislative Recognition Award

Social and Civic

- Member of Wheeler Avenue Baptist Church
- Co-Chair of the Wheeler Avenue Baptist Church building committee 2012-2019
- Member of Kappa Alpha Psi Fraternity, Inc.

In Memory of

- The Milton L. Scott Atrium in the new Cathedral 2020 was named in his honor in recognition of his perseverance and dedicated service.

Part VIII

Preserving the Dawson Legacy of Education
in
West Feliciana Parish

Preserving the "Dawson Legacy of Education in West Feliciana Parish" is an ongoing effort. For years after it closed, John S. Dawson High School sat empty on Hwy 66, waiting for the bell to ring. Eventually, covered by vegetation, the building had broken windows and collapsed ceilings. And the story would have ended except for a new generation of the Dawson family.

There was another chapter to be written in the Dawson Legacy. Ken Dawson, a grandson of John S. Dawson and son of Thomas Dawson, led the charge as about 100 members of the John S. Dawson Alumni Association/Foundation pledged to save this important West Feliciana structure. Along with Dr. Henry L. Hardy, class of 1958 and President of the Alumni Association/Foundation, the group applied for grants, launched a massive clean-up effort in 2010, and successfully had the property placed on the National Register of Historic Places in 2015.

The John S. Dawson Alumni Association/Foundation continues to work on plans for developing the property and renovating the school building. Ken Dawson explained that one day, the foundation hopes to create a parish-wide community center, an emergency preparedness site, and a park to serve the entire West Feliciana Parish population.

Photo courtesy of The JS Dawson Foundation, St. Francisville, La.

Photo courtesy of Ken Dawson, St. Francisville, La.

Notable

Ken Dawson

Business Administration

A native of St. Francisville, Ken Dawson is the son of the late Thomas Sr. and Alice Dawson, brother to Thomas Dawson of the famed Commodores, and grandson to St. Francisville's legendary Professor John Sterling Dawson.

Ken's earliest memories as a child growing up in St. Francisville shaped his adulthood. He recalled how important it was within his immediate family to maintain unity and relationships and extend assistance to others in the community through service.

As a young boy, Ken recalls the day his father, Thomas Dawson, enrolled him in the Apollo Program. This monthly mail program allowed children to learn the Apollo Mission, how to build models, and how things work. This program became the catalyst for Ken's interest in science. Later, in high school, Ken enjoyed playing all sports. Baseball and basketball were staples, but his main love was football. He excelled in football, which allowed him to receive several athletic scholarships with an opportunity to play. Still, his father decided that Ken should focus on academia. As a result, Ken received an engineering scholarship at Southern University, where he completed his B.S. degree in Mechanical Engineering.

Ken was a student in High School when he realized one personal goal. It was during a time of racial strife as the parish maintained separate waiting rooms and high school proms for Blacks and Whites. In Civics class, his introduction to the Audubon Pilgrimage project was a big deal as there was an emphasis on the antebellum homes and lifestyles of the parish. The ninth-grade class placed a significant effort into preparing for the celebration. However, Ken recalls that once it was time for the actual pilgrimage, it was as though there was no place for any Black students. "Although my entire class, both Black and White, contributed, the event excluded my Black classmates from all activities outside the classroom. There was no place for us. It was as if they had erased our history. How could we not be a part of this history?" However, what Ken gained through this experience brought enlightenment, leading Ken to ponder on a direction for his life while reminding him to continue to seek the heart of individuals.

To this day, the exclusion of Black participation in the Audubon Pilgrimage created an impression on his psyche. This very instance shaped the view of his world and his place within it.

Shortly after High School, Ken began his engineering career immediately during his first year of internship in Indianapolis, Indiana, for Detroit Diesel Allison working in Gas Turbine Research and Development.

Upon returning to Indiana after college, he was one of the first students allowed to travel with the company. Ken represented Detroit Diesel Allison at meetings and conferences within several states. "This was usual for a student to have such an opportunity; it was a defining and proud moment," Ken recalls. The following year he returned but entered another area, Aircraft Gas Turbines. During this time, about seventeen class action suits were occurring (racial issues) within the company and area-wise. At the same time, Ken was allowed to take visitors from Japan around the site to tour the company. A few weeks before Ken returned to school, he received a performance evaluation from his supervisor. To his surprise, the review was non-relevant to his role. Realizing the unjust action by his supervisor, he brought the assessment to the attention of the Vice President by having a conversation that corrected the course, resulting in an evaluation retraction statement. This experience taught Ken that no one could define him. The values learned in St. Francisville among family, and community offered him a strong sense of self and identity, which no one could take away.

After college, Ken began an accomplished career at the River Bend Nuclear Power Station. He worked for Stone and Webster Engineering during the construction phase and later with Gulf States Utilities Company for plant start-up, testing, and operation.

Within the chemical industry at Betz-Dearborn, Ken utilized his business skills as an Account Manager. He received several customer service and account management awards while sustaining accountability for over two million dollars in annual business. His ROI (Return on Investment) and Return on Environment (ROE) awards demonstrated Ken Dawsons' impeccable record for the highest quality of customer care to his clients.

Married to Barbara Washington Dawson for forty years, Ken and his wife Barbara founded several businesses. First Steps Christian Learning Center, West Feliciana Health & Fitness Center, and Strategics Group LLC. He also serves on several civic, business, government, and ministerial boards.

Ordained in the ministry in 1989, Ken Dawson serves in a leadership capacity under Pastor Calvin Veal, Jr. at the GCM Worship Center in Port Allen, La. He also serves as an Apostle to the marketplace and actively ministers to business and government leaders. He was elected to the Police Jury of West Feliciana Parish in January 2008 and served as President of West Feliciana Parish until January 2012.

For ten years, Ken served as Chief Executive Assistant for Ascension Parish. Currently, he serves as Director of Facilities Planning for the Southern University System which includes Baton Rouge, Shreveport, and New Orleans.

Ken credits the village that raised him. His parents, Thomas and Alice Roberts Dawson, were both English Majors. Both parents required their children to speak English properly and do their best no matter their paths. "The expectations of my family, being respectful, honoring my elders, and valuing all who were concerned about you and showed concern towards you contributed to my sense of self," says Ken. He continued, "Years ago, my family would sit on the front porch in the evening. Everyone would come through, from my Uncle John, Aunt Brunetta, Aunt Marion, and my parents. We would sit, talk, and tell stories about the family. These were the stories that allowed for my foundation." Ken realized the gift and legacy of his family had provided a secure foundation for his life. If his life were to be defined, it would be on his terms. Ken also understands how important it is for the next generation to understand and value our legacy.

"Very soon," Ken says, "the importance of building the John S. Dawson Center will become a community-wide center. It will become a gathering space for opportunities, meetings, and deep conversations. The John S. Dawson Community Center will become the front porch for a new generation."

And so, you see… the legacy and spirit of John Sterling Dawson is still alive. The late John S. Dawson is still teaching, just as he always did.

The John S. Dawson Alumni Association/Foundation

Photo courtesy of The Dawson Foundation, St. Francisville, La.

The John S. Dawson Alumni Association/Foundation – January 25, 2019

From left to right, Rose Mary Carter, Superintendent Hollis Milton, Nathan Price, Rufus McKnight, Governor John Bel Edwards and wife, Donna Edwards, Ken Dawson, Joyce Scott Baskin, Kevin McQuarn, Dr. Henry Hardy, Pamlynn Hardy, Katie Miller, and Calvin Miller.

The legacy and spirit of John Sterling Dawson can be attested by the chronological accomplishments and activities of the John S. Dawson Alumni Association/Foundation:

John S. Dawson alumni association/Foundation a chronology of accomplishments and activities of JSDAA/F

- December 22, 2009 - the John S. Dawson Alumni Association/Foundation Charter was amended.
- November 2010 - Massive clean-up effort at the John S. Dawson High School site.
- February 19, 2011 - the JSDAA/F held its 1st Annual Fellowship Banquet at the Hotel on the Lake in St. Francisville, Louisiana.
- February 2012 - ten members of the JSDAA/F were trained as "Mentors" by the Louisiana Office of Juvenile Justice, Baton Rouge, La.
- Friday, April 20, 2012 - the JSDAA/F held its 2nd Annual Fellowship Banquet at the Baker Civic Center in Baker, Louisiana.
- 2012 - The JSDAA/F developed a Revitalization Plan to restore the John S. Dawson High School site for development into a community center.
- April 6, 2013 - the JSDAA/F held its 3rd Annual Fellowship Banquet at the Baker Civic Center in Baker, Louisiana.
- March 15, 2014 - The JSDAA/F held its 4th Annual Fellowship Banquet at Boudreaux's Restaurant in Baton Rouge, Louisiana.
- April 25, 2015 - The JSDAA/F held its 5th Annual Fellowship Banquet at Boudreaux's Restaurant in Baton Rouge, Louisiana.
- June 15, 2015 – Through the efforts of the JSDAA/F, the John S. Dawson High School was placed on the National Register of Historic Places.
- February 28, 2016 - the JSDAA/F honored Wakefield native Major General Isaac D. Smith at Hemingbough in St. Francisville, Louisiana.
- April 2, 2016 - The JSDAA/F held its 6th Annual Fellowship Banquet at Hemingbough in St. Francisville, Louisiana.
- 2016 - The JSDAA/F requested that the John S. Dawson High School site property be transferred from the West Feliciana Parish School Board to the JSDAA/F.
- December 7, 2016 – The Office of Louisiana State Attorney General rendered a decision in our favor.

- February 23, 2017 - the West Feliciana Historical Society Museum hosted a Wine and Cheese Reception Exhibit Opening with a Black History Celebration honoring "The Dawson Legacy of Education in West Feliciana Parish."
- April 15, 2017, the JSDAA/F held its 7th Annual Fellowship Banquet at Hemingbough in St. Francisville, Louisiana.
- June 5, 2017 - the JSDAA/F received a clean-up assessment grant of $25,000.00 from Mr. Lane Grigsby at Cajun Industries.
- July 18, 2017, a taping by Louisiana Public Broadcasting was done on "The Dawson Legacy of Education in West Feliciana Parish."
- July 28, 2017 - "The Dawson Legacy of Education in West Feliciana Parish "was shown on the Louisiana Public Broadcasting.
- August 1, 2017, Minister Rufus McKnight appeared on Vimeo television discussing "The Dawson Legacy of Education in West Feliciana Parish."
- On August 15, 2017, JSDAA/F members invited guests to the St. Francisville Rotary Club Breakfast. Dr. Henry L. Hardy was the invited speaker.
- October 14, 2017 - a PowerPoint presentation on "The Dawson Legacy of Education in West Feliciana Parish" was given at the West Feliciana Parish Library.
- November 14, 2017 - the West Feliciana Parish School Board transferred the John S. Dawson High School property to the John S. Dawson Alumni Association/Foundation.
- November 16, 2017, the John S. Dawson Alumni Association/Foundation applied for a $200,000.00 Brownfield Cleanup Grant.
- January 11, 2018 - "The Dawson Legacy of Education in West Feliciana Parish" was presented at the Old Governor's Building by Dr. Henry L. Hardy.
- John S. Dawson Alumni Association/Foundation is a Non-Profit, Tax Exempt, 501 (c) (3) Organization. The JSDAA/F IRS TAX ID was reestablished on April 8, 2018.
- April 14, 2018, the JSDAA/F held its 8th Annual Fellowship Banquet at Hemingbough.
- April 15, 2018, Sunday Morning Breakfast and Sunday Church Service were held at Hemingbough in St. Francisville, Louisiana.
- October 2018 - The Flag of The United States of America was flown over the United States of America Capitol, honoring "The Dawson Legacy of Education in West Feliciana Parish." A certificate of The Architect of the Capitol and the Flag were presented to the JSDAA/F.

- January 25, 2019 - at the Governor's Manson, the John S. Dawson Alumni Association Foundation tells Governor John Bel Edwards about its goal of establishing a community center.
- February 21, 2019 - the John S. Dawson Alumni Association/Foundation held a Black History event at the West Feliciana Historical Society Museum in St. Francisville, Louisiana.
- March 16, 2019 - Videographer Kevin McQuarn, of Fantomlight Production and West Feliciana High School Students created a documentary for the John S. Dawson Alumni Association Foundation.
- April 6, 2019 - the JSDAA/F held its 9th Annual Fellowship Banquet at Hemingbough.
- April 7, 2019 - Sunday Morning Breakfast and Sunday Church Service were held at Hemingbough in St. Francisville, Louisiana.
- August 16, 2019 - the JSDAA/F had a presentation and reception at the West Feliciana Historical Society Museum. Pictures and other items were presented for the exhibit.
- November 1, 2019 - the JSDAA/F applied for a Louisiana Capital Outlay grant of $5,285,000.00. The Capital Outlay grant will renovate the John S. Dawson High school site into a parish-wide community center and Emergency Preparedness site.
- October 9, 2020 – Superintendent Hollis Milton, Ken Dawson, Mattie Hardy, and Henry Hardy met with State Senator Glen Womack to discuss the vision of the John S. Dawson Alumni Association Foundation. Discussed was the potential for the Capital Outlay project.
- On October 14, 2020, the JSDAA/F reapplied for a Louisiana Capital Outlay grant for $5,285,000.00. The Capital Outlay grant will renovate the John S. Dawson High Scholl site into a parish-wide community center and Emergency Preparedness site.
- February 8, 2021 - the JSDAA/F agreed with Fantomlight production to produce a Dawson Novel on "The Dawson Legacy of Education in West Feliciana Parish."
- November 4, 2021 - the JSDAA/F reapplied for a Louisiana Capital Outlay grant for $5,285.000.00. The Capital Outlay grant will renovate the John S. Dawson High School site into a parish-wide community center and Emergency Preparedness site.
- December 16, 2021 - the JSDAA/F held its annual Christmas luncheon at the Lagniappe Restaurant in Zachary, Louisiana.
- April 9, 2022 - the JSDAA/F received a draft and color prints of the Dawson Novel from Fantomlight production.
- April 23, 2022 - the JADAA/F host its first Faith-Based meeting at the Catholic Student Center on the Southern University campus in Baton Rouge, Louisiana.

- May 7, 2022 - the JSDAA/F host its second Faith-Based meeting at the Catholic Student Center on the Southern University Campus in Baton Rouge, Louisiana.
- May 16, 2022 - the JSDAA/F established a Webpage with twenty (20) relevant items, including the history of John S. Dawson High School from 1951 through 1969.
- June 4, 2022 - the JSDAA/F host its third Faith-Based meeting at the Catholic Student Center on the Southern University Campus in Baton Rouge, Louisiana.

From left to right: Mattie Wilcox Dunbar, Annette Mackie Keith, Rufus McKnight, Vincent Smith, Joyce Scott Baskin, Samuel Mitchell, Nathan D. Price, Ken Dawson, Dr. Henry Hardy, Willie Stevens, Joseph Cummings, Rose Mary Carter, and Calvin Miller.

THIS IS TO CERTIFY THAT THE

JOHN S. DAWSON HIGH SCHOOL

WAS ENTERED INTO THE

NATIONAL REGISTER OF HISTORIC PLACES

UNDER THE PROVISIONS OF THE

NATIONAL HISTORIC PRESERVATION ACT OF 1966

15TH DAY OF JUNE 2015

KEEPER OF THE NATIONAL REGISTER

LIEUTENANT GOVERNOR

STATE HISTORIC PRESERVATION OFFICER

Through the efforts of the JSDAA/F, the John S. Dawson High School was placed on the National Register of Historic Places.

Photo courtesy of the J.S.Dawson Foundation

From left to right: Mr. Hollis Milton-Superintendent of West Feliciana School District, State Senator Glen Womack, Mrs. Mattie Hardy, Dr. Henry Hardy, and Ken Dawson.

Photo courtesy of the J.S.Dawson Foundation

From left to right: Mr. Ken Dawson, Mrs. Dot Temple, Dr. Henry Hardy, and Mr. Cliff Deal.

Photo courtesy of The Dawson Foundation, St. Francisville, La.

From left to right: Dr. Henry L. Hardy and Major General Issac D. Smith.

Photo courtesy of The Dawson Foundation, St. Francisville, La.

From left to right: Thomas Dawson and Walter Orange of the Commodores, Dr. Henry Hardy and Ken Dawson of the Dawson Foundation.

Part IX

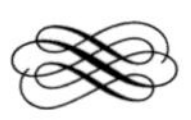

Summary by Dr. Henry Hardy

Notable People of Color – St. Francisville, Louisiana

The exclusion of People of Color in the history of West Feliciana Parish is a typical example of the exclusion of People of Color in the history of the south. Yet, People of Color from Louisiana have made significant contributions to many professions: This includes the following: Actor; Tyler Perry. Baseball; Lou Brock. Basketball; Carl Malone, Willis Reed, Bill Russell. Football; Fred Dean, Buck Buchannan, Ernie Ladd, Coach Eddie Robinson, Doug Williams. Journalist; Don Lemon. Lawyer; Johnny Cochran. Politics; Andrew Young. Military; Lieutenant General Russell L. Honore', Major General Isaac D. Smith. Music; Mahalia Jackson, and others.

American history should include the good, the bad, and the ugly. Some of America's stories may be offensive to some people, but it should still be presented. It is also in my opinion that all Americans should become familiar with the following: The German Coast Uprising (1811) in Laplace, Louisiana; the Tulsa Race Massacre (1921) in Tulsa, Oklahoma; The rape of Recy Taylor (1944) in Abbeville, Alabama; and The Florida School for Boys (1955) in Okeechobee, Florida.

Institutional racism, the socioeconomic system, existing medical issues, less access to health care, and work in unstable jobs, are factors that disproportionately hurt People of Color more than others. Compound the aforementioned with cases like the lynching of Emmitt Till in Mississippi, the brutal beating of Rodney King in Los Angeles, the killing of Treyvon Martin in Florida, the killing of Eric Gardner in New York, the murder of Michael Brown in Missouri, the murder of John Crawford in Ohio, the Murder of Dontre Hamilton in Wisconsin, the murder of Ezell Ford in California, the murder of Ahmaud Arbery in Georgia, the killing of Breonne Taylor in Louisville, the killing of George Floyd in Minnesota, and the killing of Rayshard Brooks in Georgia.

Institutional racism (also known as systemic racism) "is a form of racism embedded as a normal practice within society or an organization. It can lead to such issues as discrimination in criminal justice, employment, housing, health care, political power, and education, among other issues." Institutional racism must be addressed before America can move forward with peace and justice for all citizens.

Congressman John Lewis (1938-2020) stated that "combating segregation is one thing, dealing with racism is another." Attitudes are harder to target than behaviors. It is my opinion this is the reason racism is harder to abolish than segregation. Ultimately, though, unless racist attitudes are annihilated, no amount of effort will permanently establish equal rights.

Congressman John Lewis: "like his mentor, the Rev., Dr. Martin Luther King, Jr., the long-standing Congressman was an ordained Black Baptist Minister. It meant that he not only knew how to phrase legislative briefs but also ancient biblical texts and extrapolate wisdom from them to address social issues with great urgency. For Christians like Lewis, preaching, though not an end itself, is a means by which God reminds society of God's concern for community wellness, life, human dignity, and freedom in a less-than-perfect world. Preaching, in their understanding, tells the truth about suffering in the context of fear and death. Ultimately it declares evil and the truth about suffering in the context of fear and death. Ultimately it declares that evil and despair have an appointed end. Because of this, as John Lewis said in his posthumously penned op-ed: each of us has a moral obligation to stand up, speak up, and speak out."[15]

Photo courtesy of Dr. Henry L. Hardy

Notable

Dr. Henry L. Hardy, author of *Notable People of Color – St. Francisville, Louisiana,* founder of the John S. Dawson Foundation, and past president and co-founder of the John S. Dawson Alumni Association/Foundation Charter, St. Francisville, La.

(December 10, 1940 – March 22, 2023)

Dr. Henry L. Hardy was a 1958 graduate of John S. Dawson High School. After serving in the U.S. Air Force, he received a Bachelor of Science in Mathematics from Southern University. Dr. Hardy relocated to Hartford, Connecticut, where he continued his educational training by obtaining a master's in mathematics from Central Connecticut State University, an advanced degree from the University of Hartford Connecticut in Mathematics and Administration/Supervision, and a Doctorate in Mathematics from Temple University in Philadelphia, Pennsylvania.

From 1979 through 2001, Dr. Hardy received grants from the National Science Foundation, The William Penn Foundation, Minority Science Improvement Program, United States Department of Education, Pennsylvania Education Department, the United States Department of Energy and in May 2001 a $2.5 million grant from the National Science Foundation for a "Program for Excellence in Science, Mathematics, and Computer Technology."

In addition to serving as a professor of Mathematics and Administrator at Cheyney University of Pennsylvania and Southern University at New Orleans, Dr. Hardy received grants from the National Science Foundation, Minority Science Improvement Program, William Penn Foundation, United States Department of Education, Pennsylvania Education Department, and the United States Department of Energy.

After retiring from Cheyney University of Pennsylvania, Dr. Hardy moved from Pennsylvania to New Orleans, La. In 1994 for thirteen years, he was employed at Southern University of New Orleans (SUNO), where he was a tenured Professor of Mathematics, Director of "Program for Excellence, Mathematics, and Computer Technology," and Vice Chancellor for Academic Affairs.

Dr. Hardy taught mathematics at Capital Junior High School in Baton Rouge, Louisiana and Weaver High School in Hartford, Connecticut. He was also a Commissioner for the South-Central Planning and Development Commission.

Awards

- The President's Award for Academic Excellence – Cheyney University
- The Commonwealth of Pennsylvania Distinguished Faculty Award
- The Commonwealth of Pennsylvania Certificate for Exceptional Academic Service
- The Marcus Foster Award for Outstanding Educators – by Educators Roundtable, Inc.

- Who's Who Among American Teachers and Educators for 2006-2007
- Grant Awards (1979 – 2001)
- The National Science Foundation
- The Minority Science Improvement Program
- The William Penn Foundation
- The United States Department of Education
- The Pennsylvania Education Department
- The United States Department of Energy

Professional Boards

- Commissioner for the South-Central Planning and Development Commission (includes the following parishes: Assumption, St. Charles, St. James, St. John the Baptist, Lafourche, St. Mary, and Terrebonne).
- Community and Civic Boards
- Chairperson of the Board of Trustees - St. Michael Baptist Church
- Co-Founder of the St. John the Baptist Parish Action Group
- Co-founder and past president of the John S. Dawson Alumni Association/Foundation
- Past member of Tulane Baptist Church – New Orleans

Additional Content
for
Notable People of Color – St. Francisville, Louisiana

The following excerpts are from local Louisiana news sources. Please note, all excerpts are unedited and in their original form.

Civil Rights Suit Filed by Minister-

Baton Rouge, (AP) - A Negro minister has filed a federal court suit here under the 1960 civil rights act against two officials of West Feliciana Parish. Carter's petition claims he was denied his civil rights when he and Rev. Rudolph Davis went to the voter registration office on Aug. 10

The Rev. Joseph Carter, in his $100,000 suit against Sheriff William C. Percy, Jr. and Voter Registrar Fletcher Harvey, claimed Thursday that he was denied the right to vote and falsely arrested.

Sheriff Percy was unavailable immediately for comment.

Harvey, reached at his St. Francisville home said, "as far as a suit against me, he's all wet."

Counsel for Carter said Negros make up 66 percent of the population in West Feliciana Parish, according to the last census, and there are no Negroes registered to vote. Counsel for Carter said the attempt by the two Negros to register may have been the first of its kind since Reconstruction Days.

-The Town Talk (Alexandria, Louisiana) 20 Sept 1963, Fri
Newspapers by Ancestry.com

The Town Talk (Alexandria, Louisiana) · 20 Sep 1963, Fri · Page 12

Four Negros Registered as CORE Drive Begins-

The voter registration drive being conducted by the Congress of Racial Equality in parishes in the Baton Rouge area got underway in West Feliciana Parish on Thursday of last week and at press time Wednesday four negroes had successfully met qualifications and been registered.

A school bus load of negroes reported to be mostly from the northern part of the parish arrived at the Courthouse shortly after 9 a.m. It was reported that there were 43 negroes on the bus. The first negro registered early in the afternoon on Thursday and three more registered Friday.

Also reported to be among the federal officials on the scene was a man identified as Frank Dunbaugh, assistant U.S. attorney general in charge of civil rights.

-St. Francisville Democrat (St. Francisville, Louisiana) 24 Oct. 1963, Thur
Newspapers by Ancestry.com

St. Francisville Democrat (St. Francisville, Louisiana) · 24 Oct 1963, Thu · Page 1

Minister Who Sued Sheriff Registered-

ST. FRANCISVILLE, LA. -

A minister ignored a group of threatening white men here last Thursday and became West Feliciana Parish's first Negro registered voter since Reconstruction Days.

The Rev. Joseph Carter entered the side door of the historic courthouse, the front entrance having been blocked by angry whites, and successfully passed the voter registration test Thursday afternoon as Justice Department and FBI agents watched.

Three other Negroes were registered on Friday bringing the total number to four Negro voters last weekend. They are Nathaniel Smith, a 66-year-old farmer; Ernest Morgan, 54, also a farmer, and Handy Berry, a 22-year-old unemployed hod-carrier.

"FOUR OF TWELVE"

The two-day total was 12 Negroes being given the voter registration test with four succeeding.

Until the Rev. Mr. Carter registered, West Feliciana and Tensas were the only two remaining parishes in the state without a registered Negro voter.

Ronnie Moore, Baton Rouge, field secretary for the Congress of Racial Equality, last Wednesday notified Justice Departments agents that Negroes would apply for registration here Thursday morning. He met with Frank Dunbar, a member of the legal staff of the Justice Dept., directly across the street in front of the Grace Episcopal Church about 10 minutes before the registrar's office opened at 9 a.m.

Accompanied by Dunbar Moore entered the courthouse and asked for District Attorney Richard Kilbourne. Later the vote registrar, Fletcher Harvey, agreed to take registrants from a list as submitted by the group in the order in which their names appeared.

IGNORES THREATS

As the Rev. Mr. Carter approached the side entrance one of a group of white men warned him he would be emasculated if he entered the building. The Rev. Mr. Carter walked on, apparently unhearing.

The minister was one of 43 Negros who arrived at the courthouse in a school bus. It was the first mass voter registration attempt here by CORE. Six applied for registration. All but Rev. Carter were told they failed Thursday.

While Rev. Carter was in the registrar's office, a girl CORE worker entered the courthouse hall. When she walked toward a water fountain, an unidentified white man shouted:

"You can't drink out of that; if you do I'll cut your guts out!"

Parish authorities intervened and led the man outside, as the girl left the building without drinking.

-The Louisiana Weekly (New Orleans, Louisiana) · 26 Oct 1963, Sat
Newspapers by Ancestry.com

The Louisiana Weekly (New Orleans, Louisiana) · 26 Oct 1963, Sat · Page 1

U.S. Charges Violation of Vote Rights
Federal Suit Asks End to Restrictions in West Feliciana-

NEW ORLEANS (AP) - The Justice Department charged Tuesday Negroes still face unlawful discrimination in West Feliciana Parish, La., where it said a few Negros registered to vote this month for the first time in almost 60 years.

The charges were made in a suit filed in U.S. District Court.

Atty. Gen. Robert F. Kennedy said the complaint asked that Registrar Fletcher Harvey be ordered to end unreasonable restrictions against Negros voter registration.

The suit charged that Negros seeking to register were required to prove their residence either by precise documentation or by the statements of two voters already registered in their precinct.

In addition, the suit said, processing of Negro applications was delayed unreasonably and more stringent requirements were applied to Negro applicants than whites.

Until Oct. 17, Negro applicants had been required to produce two registered voters to vouch for their identity, the suit said, adding that until that time no Negroes had been registered for many years.

-The Times (Shreveport, Louisiana) - 30 Oct. 1963, Wed
Newspapers by Ancestry.com

The Times (Shreveport, Louisiana) · 30 Oct 1963, Wed · Page 9

<u>Negro Voter Registration Drive Continues Here-</u>

The Congress of Racial Equality continued their Negro voter registration drive this week, and at press time Wednesday, a total of 11 Negros had been registered to vote.

Seven Negros had registered as of last Wednesday.

The CORE drive started in this parish on October 17 and Negros have been attempting to register on about three days out of each week.

-St. Francisville Democrat (St. Francisville, Louisiana)* * *7 Nov 1963, Thur
Newspapers by Ancestry.com

St. Francisville Democrat (St. Francisville, Louisiana) · 7 Nov 1963, Thu · Page 1

CORE Voices Complaints in Two Parishes-

ST. FRANCISVILLE, (AP) - A Congress of Racial Equality (CORE) field worker complained Thursday 40 Negroes were turned away from the voter registrar's office here and 15 at Clinton, 50 miles eastward.

Atty. Gen. Jack Gremillion said registrars in 21 parishes involved in a recent federal court order were advised to comply, even though the state has appealed.

Both registrars' offices in the two rural parishes were targets of CORE Negro drives before the Democratic first and second primaries.

Registration books opened again last Monday, 30 days before the March 3 general election, when they will close again.

Ronnie Moore, Negro field secretary for CORE, said the 55 Negroes were blocked.

Gremillion, commenting on the development said, "We made a copy of the federal order to the 21 parishes and we sent it to every registrar of voters and every district attorney and assistant district attorney. We told them we suggested they comply. We have appealed this federal court order. However, we have suggested to registrars to comply with it until the matter is finally settled."

-The Times (Shreveport, Louisiana) - 17 Jan 1964, Fri
Newspapers by Ancestry.com

The Times (Shreveport, Louisiana) · 17 Jan 1964, Fri · Page 16

Supreme Court Agrees to Hear "Voter" Arguments-

WASHINGTON (UPI) - The State of Louisiana will ask the U.S. Supreme Court next fall the overturn a lower-court ruling striking down the state's constitutional interpretation voter registration test.

The high court agreed Monday to hear arguments during its next term, starting in October.

A three-judge federal court in New Orleans voided the portion of the Louisiana constitution providing for the test last November 27 by 2-1 vote.

The court's order also enjoined 21 parishes from using a newer multiple choice citizenship test for voter registration.

The constitutional test required voter applicants to "understand and give a reasonable interpretation" of any section of the state or federal constitutions.

Registrars Fletcher Harvey of West Feliciana Parish and Henry Earl Palmer of East Feliciana closed their offices the same month the order was issued. They claimed state law required the constitutional test and they could not operate under the federal court order without violating state law.

However, the U.S. 5th circuit Court of Appeals ordered Harvey and Palmer Monday to open their offices immediately and begin registering voters.

The Bastrop Daily Enterprise (Bastrop, Louisiana) - 23 Jun 1964, Tues
Newspapers by Ancestry.com

The Bastrop Daily Enterprise (Bastrop, Louisiana) · 23 Jun 1964, Tue · Page 1

West Feliciana
U.S. Files Its First Voter Intimidation Suit in Louisiana-

Baton Rouge (AP)- The federal government charged Monday that landowners in West Feliciana Parish-just north of this capital city-have evicted from their lifelong homes Negro sharecroppers and tenant farmers who registered to vote.

In its first voter intimidation suit under the 1965 Voting Rights Act, the Justice Department sought court orders to end interference with Negroes seeking to exercise their right to vote.

Atty. Gen. Nicholas Katzenbach filed suit in federal district court at New Orleans last Friday, asking that a permanent injunction be granted against eight landowners, including the parish voting registrar.

The suit was transferred Monday to the Baton Rouge division of the southern district federal court of Louisiana. A hearing was set for Thursday.

The Justice Department said in Washington the action against the Louisiana landowners was the first of its kind.

Named as defendants were the registrar, Fletcher Harvey, Edward I. Daniel, Jordon Truitt, John Spillman, R. Harry Daniel Jr., B. Harrison Barrow and Daniel and Truitt, Inc., a farming firm.

At St. Francisville, the seat of justice for West Feliciana Parish, Registrar Harvey declined comment. The other defendants could not be reached for comment.

State Atty. Gen. Jack P.F. Gremillion issued a statement critical of Harvey and said his office would not defend the registrar in court.

"Mr. Harvey has never consulted me about any of the operations of his office," said Gremillion. "Apparently he has been depending on local counsel and advice. I didn't give him any advice upon which he acted.

TOLD TO COMPLY

"In fact, I told parish registrars, right after the civil rights bill was enacted, to comply with the law until such time that it might be declared unconstitutional.

"Apparently, Mr. Harvey didn't follow my advice and sought his own counsel.

"I'm not responsible for the predicament that he is in. He caused it of his own accord. As far as I'm concerned he can depend upon his local advisers to defend him in the matter."

Federal voting registrars have been sent to St. Francisville. It was not immediately known how many Negros they have put on the voting rolls of the tiny parish.

The Justice Department said that Harvey's office registered only 60 Negros out of 2,700 eligible by Aug. 6 when the voting rights bill was signed. From then until Sept. 1, 450 were registered by Harvey kept his office open only 2 1/2 days until Oct. 1 and then closed it completely.

"I have lived on this plantation for 67 years," Henry Cummings a tenant farmer, wrote in a typical affidavit accompanying the Louisiana suit. When he registered to vote, Cummings said, Registrar Fletcher Harvey warned him he might be evicted. And, Cummings said, he soon received a terse letter from the farming firm of Daniel & Truitt, also a defendant. It said:

"Dear Henry: This letter is to give you notice that our crop year is up and we want you to move by Jan. 1, 1966."

The department filed more than a dozen affidavits from Negro farmers. Most recounted threats and eviction notices that followed their decisions to register: some said they saved their family homes by changing their minds and staying away from the registrar's office.

By the end of 1963 none of West Feliciana Parish's 2,700 eligible Negroes was registered to vote and nearly all of its 1,400 eligible whites were registered, the department said. By Aug. 6, 1965, when the voting law was signed, some 60 Negroes had registered: 450 more signed up.

In September, the department said, Harvey cut to 2 1/2 days a week the registration time in his office and 220 more Negros registered. Harvey closed the office completely in October, and on October 29, Katzenbach designated the parish for the appointment of federal voting examiners under the new law.

1,725 REGISTERED

Since the examiners opened their office Nov. 3, they have listed more than 1,000 Negroes as eligible to vote and about 1,725 are now registered in the parish.

From October on, the complaints said, the Negroes who registered here have been subjected to a variety of economic penalties-usually the termination of long-standing sharecropping and tenant farming agreements.

From one plantation alone, the department said, seven sharecroppers and cash renters certified they had been given eviction letters after they had registered. But another Negro, who said he was worried that registration might mean the loss of his home, said he did not register and received no eviction notice.

In a related development, the department announced that Attorney General Nicholas Katzenbach will carry his get-out-the-vote message personally to southern Negroes for the first time in a Jan. 2 visit to Mobile, Ala. In his Emancipation Day appearance, he will establish a sort of precedent: no attorney general has ever addressed an all-Negro gathering in the South.

Tuesday, Dec. 21, 1965 - The Shreveport Times
Newspapers by Ancestry.com

The Times (Shreveport, Louisiana) · 21 Dec 1965, Tue · Page 18

Christmas: Louisiana Style-
Evection Victims Holiday Cheerless

Mrs. Edna London and her 11 children of St. Francisville, La., did not have a very merry Christmas this year.

Why?

Because she registered to vote.

For this, Mrs. London was evicted from the four-room house on the 100 acre plantation farm on which she has lived and worked for the past 20 years.

"I wasn't able to do a thing for Christmas for the children," she said. Normally, while it may be pretty skimpy, at least I can do something."

Mrs. London was not alone in her plight. At least 26 other Negro families, including over 60 children in rural West Feliciana parish (it means happy Land) have also received notice of eviction. All because they registered to vote.

Mrs. London's story is somewhat typical of the evicted families. Her landlord, parish registrar Fletcher Harvey, told her he did not wish to farm the land anymore. This despite the fact her sweet potato crop has been the best ever the past two years. Harvey offered her the alternative of leaving or paying $25 a month rent.

Mrs. London could not afford the monthly payment. In addition she quit her part-time job as a housekeeper because of illness and because she expected to be fired anyway for registering. She has since applied for work at nearby East Louisiana Hospital, and if accepted will be able to support her family.

Leonard Peck, his wife and four children have also been evicted. Mr. and Mrs. Peck registered to vote when a federal registrar come into the parish on October 29, 1965. Several weeks later he was told to "get off" his farm by the landlord.

The Pecks will be moving into an old church which has been torn down and reassembled on land owned by one of the church's deacons. Peck has been a farmer all his life but with no land to cultivate he'll have to give up farming. He said he would try and work as a laborer.

The Louisiana Weekly (New Orleans, Louisiana) - 8 Jan 1966, Sat
Newspapers by Ancestry.com

The Louisiana Weekly (New Orleans, Louisiana) · 8 Jan 1966, Sat · Page 17

First Black Registered Voters in West Feliciana Parish – October 17, 1963

Mr. Eddie Baker
Mrs. Maria Turner Baker
Ms. Matleane Blackmore
Mr. John Brandon
Mr. Feltus Brown
Mr. John Henry Brown
Reverend Joe Carter
Mrs. Helen Hamilton
Mr. Johnny Hamilton
Mrs. Mary Hamilton
Mr. Norvel Hamilton
Mr. Bill Harris
Mr. Thomas Harris, Sr.
Mr. Andrew Jenkins
Mr. George Johnson
Mr. Steve Johnson
Mr. Albert McKenzie
Mr. Ledell Mackie
Mr. Raymond Minor
Mr. William Minor
Mr. Ernest Morgan
Mrs. Susie Morgan
Reverend George Norflin
Mr. James Paines
Ms. Maple Pate
Ms. Rose Pate
Mr. Jesse Perkins

Reverend Quint Quire
Mr. Nathanial Smith
Mrs. Sallie Smith
Mr. Vincent Smith
Reverend Jessie Taylor
Mr. Eddie Woods

Successful Black Farmers in West Feliciana Parish 1940 – 1970

West Feliciana Parish had many black families that were successful farmers within the parish. To the best of my ability, this list includes the following families:

- Mr. Adolph Cavalier
- Mr. Major Cavalier
- Mr. General Colbert
- Mr. Commodore Goodman
- Mr. William Hamilton
- Mr. Thomas Harris
- Mr. Wesley Harris
- Mr. Nathaniel Hawthorne
- Mr. Robert Johnson
- Mr. Sullivan Johnson
- Mr. Ledell Mackie
- Mr. Willie Mackie
- Mr. Harry Minor
- Mr. William Minor
- Mr. Ernest Morgan
- Mr. Cain Nettle
- Mr. Lyndall Pate
- Mr. Matthew Pate
- Mr. Samuel Pate
- Mr. Elisha Polk
- Mr. Louis Polk
- Mr. George Roach
- Mr. Harry Rowan
- Mr. Willie Bennett Scott, II
- Mr. Robert Sterling
- Mr. Vincent Welch

To the best of my recollection, during the period of 1949-1958, the following Black families lived in the heart (town) of St. Francisville. It was during this time I met schoolmates and life-long friends. They include:

Willard and Beatrice Anderson & family
Joseph and Bertha Armstrong & family
Phil and Amelia Bailey & family
James and Fairfax Bailey & family
Louis and Georgia Bailey & family
Zedrick and Lucille Bailey & family
Leonard Ball & family
Coleman and Florence Barrow & family
Joseph Bennett & family
Jerry and Mitalda Brooks & family
Leon and Rosalee Brown & family
Arthur and Sarah Brown & family
Ernest and Viola Butler & family
Willie and Rose Bruce & family
Leon and Ruby Cage & family
Harrison and Gertrude Callahan & family
Fred and Amelia Cambell & family
Ezekial and Alme Canty & family
Alex and Matilda Carter & family
Alvin and Alice Carter & family
Bessie Carter & family
Luvenia Cuttlow & family
Matthew and Horan Davis & family
John. S. and Corine Dawson & family
John and Fredonia Dawson & family
Thomas and Alice Dawson & family
Ellen Douglas & family

Jim and Parfina Duncan & family
Alfred and Carrie Forman & family
Johnny and Emma Mae Gice & family
Belle P. Gilmore & family
Derby and Roxie Gray & family
David Grimes & family
Eugene and Doris Givens & family
Samuel and Rosina Guess & family
Alice Gullage & family
Silas and Elnora Hardy & family
William and Katharine Hoffman & family
Andrew and Sallie Jackson & family
Frank and Sally Jackson & family
Shirley Jackson & family
Iramount and Julia Ann Jackson & family
Joseph and Natlee Johnson & family
Max and Julia Estell Johnson Maurice Jones & family
Oscar and Edna King & family
Ronald and Peggy King & family
Felton and Mary Lee & family
Samuel and Florence Lee & family
James and Gertrude Leonard & family
Isaiah and Irene Mitchell & family
Sarah Mitchell & family
James and Sarah Monroe & family
James Morgan & family
James and Pauline Morrison & family
William and Mary Netter & family
Dorothy Raspberry & family
Jerry and Azarene Reed & family
Charles and Amelia Roach & family
Oscar and Louise Robinson & family

Jimmy Rogers & family
William and Bernadene Rogers & family
Alvin and Roselee Sims & family
Samuel and Geraldine Smothers & family
Ike and Alpine Snowden & family
Jean Spikes & family
William and Margaret Sterling & family
Fred and Rose Nell Sterling & family
Nelson and Mariah Stevens & family
Walter and Barbara Stevens & family
Woodrow and Lucy Stevens & family
William Taylor & family
Howard Temple & family Miles Temple & family
Netta Mae Thomas & family
Johnny Tyler & family
Tudia Tyler & family
Andrew and Alice Mae Vessels & family
Edward and Velma Whitaker & family
Felton White & family
Mariah White & family
Geraldine Wicker & family
Arthur Williams & family
Dave and Viola Williams &
family Jim and Emma Williams & family
John and Bertha Williams & family
Marie Williams & family
Horace and Emma Jean Williams & family
Vincent and Matilda Williams & family
Earl Williams & family
Jim Willis & family
Otis and Emma Wilson & family
Jimmy Wood & family

About the Author

The late Dr. Henry L. Hardy was married to Mattie M. Hardy, and together they built their life in LaPlace, Louisiana.

They have three children, Louis C. Hardy (deceased), Pamlynn Hardy, and Turland Malone (Mattie Malone Hardy), two grandchildren, Justin Roland and Rogie L. Magee, Jr., and two great-grandchildren, Rogie L. Magee, III and Khenzi A. Magee.

His hobbies included reading, watching mysteries, western movies, and traveling. In addition, Dr. Hardy was an avid sports watcher of all kinds and loved to attend live sports when possible.

He loved his dear ole alma mater, "Southern University," and enjoyed all opportunities to watch Southern University and Grambling State University football teams play.

Dr. Hardy was the author of *"Notable People of Color – St. Francisville, Louisiana,"* organizer and visionary for the children's book, *"The Dawson Legacy - an Inspirational Story of Hope and Determination,"* creator of the historical map, *"When St. Francisville, La. Was People of Color,"* founder of the John S. Dawson Foundation, and past president and co-founder of the John S. Dawson Alumni Association/Foundation Charter, St. Francisville, La.

Passionate and dedicated, a fierce leader, and a tireless contributor, Dr. Henry L. Hardy was an example of excellence for all who knew him. His legacy will be felt for generations to come.

When asked "why you are doing something," Dr. Hardy's most famous response would be, "because I can."

Photo courtesy of the J.S. Dawson Foundation

Governor John Bel Edwards and Dr. Henry L. Hardy Governor's Mansion - January 25, 2019

Acknowledgements

I thank all who contributed to the publication of this book. First, I give thanks to God for granting me faith, patience, and endurance to complete this book.

My heartfelt appreciation goes to my wife and friend, Mattie Hardy, for the original cover and graphics concept. Throughout our marriage, Mattie has supported me in all my ventures and activities, and I am eternally grateful.

A thank you to my daughter, Pamlynn Hardy, for her assistance in organizing and proofreading the manuscript during its initial stage.

To my editor, Tonya Scott Wyandon. I am positive that the manuscript would not have moved forward without the knowledge, experience, persistence, dedication, and passion of Tonya.

To the AuthorHouse Publishing staff including Mae Genson, Jessie Dean, Aubrey Siever, and Melanie Lear.

Thank you to my brother-in Christ, Vincent Smith, for his contributions and weekly discussion on family, church, and educational activities.

Thank you to the following for your extensive and invaluable contributions pertaining to family history: Mr. Ken Dawson, for your contributions pertaining to your grandfather, John Sterling Dawson, and your support, John Sterling Dawson, Ms. Lucy Miller for her contribution on the Dawson family history, and Vincent Smith for his contribution on the Smith family history.

To my childhood friend, Mr. Willie Stevens for his assistance in completing the Map of St. Francisville and Rufus McKnight for your support.

Many thanks to the dedicated members of the John S. Dawson Alumni Association/Foundation including the following: Joyce Scott Baskin, Rose Mary Carter, Joseph Cummings, Ken Dawson, Mattie Wilcox Dunbar, Annette Mackie Keith, Rufus McKnight, Calvin Miller, Samuel Mitchell, Nathan D. Price, Vincent Smith, and Willie Stevens.

"Whatever you do, do it so well that people looking on will feel that the task was reserved especially for you by God himself."

– Benjamin E. Mays
(1894-1984)

Endnotes

1 Bedingfield, G. (n.d.). *Charlie Wilcox*. Baseball's Greatest Sacrifice. Retrieved July 24, 2022, from https://www.

2 baseballsgreatestsacrifice.com/biographies/wilcox charlie.html

3 *Buddy Guy Historical Marker*. (n.d.). Retrieved July 24, 2022, from https://www.hmdb.org/m.asp?m=127700

4 Contributors to Wikimedia projects. (2022a, April 5). *Isaac D. Smith*. Wikipedia. https://en.wikipedia.org/wiki/Isaac D. Smith 4 Contributors to Wikimedia projects. (2022b, June 17). *John R.* Wikipedia. https://en.wikipedia.org/wiki/John R.

5 Contributors to Wikimedia projects. (2022c, June 29). *Leland College*. Wikipedia. https://en.wikipedia.org/wiki/Leland College

6 *Historical Society features John S. Dawson legacy exhibit at museum*. (n.d.). West Feliciana Historical Society. Retrieved July 24, 2022, from https://www.westfelicianahistory.org/news/historical-society-features-john-s-dawson-legacy-exhibit-at-museum

7 *Home - Saint Francisville, LA*. (n.d.). West Feliciana Historical Society. Retrieved July 23, 2022, from https://www.westfelicianahistory.org/

8 Jackson, D. (2020, June 10). West Feliciana Historical Society permanently cancels Audubon Pilgrimage after petition claims festival... *WAFB*. https://www.wafb.com/2020/06/10/west-feliciana-historical-society-permanently-cancels-audubon-pilgrimageafter-petition-claims-festival-glosses-over-slavery/

9 jgolebiowski. (n.d.). *LA _West feliciana parish _john S. Dawson high school* .

10 *Leland College, Baker Louisiana*. (n.d.). Historic Structures. Retrieved July 23, 2022, from http://historic-structures.com/la/baker/leland_ college.php

11 Mchie, B. (2020, May 16). *Leland College is Founded*. African American Registry. https://aaregistry.org/story/leland-college-founded/

12 *Our beginnings*. (n.d.). St. Francisville Funeral Home. Retrieved July 24, 2022, from https://www.stfrancisvillefuneralhome.com/ history

13 *The Elders Speak: the West Feliciana Parish African American oral history project*. (n.d.). Retrieved July 23, 2022, from https://www. louisianafolklife.org/LT/Articles Essays/WestFeliciana8.html

14 *Thomas Dawson*. (n.d.). Visual & Performing Arts. Retrieved July 24, 2022, from https://vapa.uccs.edu/index/music/faculty/dawson

15 (N.d.). Retrieved July 24, 2022, from https://fzot.rnsmessina.it/sermons-by-black-preachers-free.html 16 1963, B. A. (n.d.). *Birth of a Voter (CORE reprint, of Ebony Magazine article).*

16 CORE, J. F. (n.d.). *Louisiana Story, 1963. CORE pamphlet*. (2015, June 22). SU Ag Center chancellor Leodrey Williams to retire after half a century. HBCU Buzz. https://hbcubuzz.com/2015/06/su-ag-center-chancellor-leodrey-williams-to-retire-after-half-a-century/

Works Cited

Bedingfield, G. (n.d.). *Charlie Wilcox*. Baseball's Greatest Sacrifice. Retrieved July 24, 2022, from https:// www.baseballsgreatestsacrifice.com/biographies/wilcox_ charlie.html

Buddy Guy Historical Marker. (n.d.). Retrieved July 24, 2022, from https://www.hmdb.org/m.asp?m=127700 Contributors to Wikimedia projects. (2022a, April 5). *Isaac D. Smith*. Wikipedia. https://en.wikipedia. org/wiki/Isaac D. Smith

Contributors to Wikimedia projects. (2022b, June 17). *John R.* Wikipedia. https://en.wikipedia.org/wiki/ John R.

Contributors to Wikimedia projects. (2022c, June 29). *Leland College*. Wikipedia. https://en.wikipedia. org/wiki/Leland College

Historical Society features John S. Dawson legacy exhibit at museum. (n.d.). West Feliciana Historical Society. Retrieved July 24, 2022, from https://www.westfelicianahistory.org/news/ historical-society-features-john-s-dawson-legacy-exhibit-at-museum.

Home - Saint Francisville, LA. (n.d.). West Feliciana Historical Society. Retrieved July 23, 2022, from https://www.westfelicianahistory.org/

Jackson, D. (2020, June 10). West Feliciana Historical Society permanently cancels Audubon Pilgrimage after petition claims festival... *WAFB*. https://www.wafb.com/2020/06/10/west-feliciana-historicalsociety-permanently-cancels-audubon-pilgrimage-after-petition-claims-festival-glosses-over-slavery/

jgolebiowski. (n.d.). *LA_ West Feliciana parish john S. Dawson high school* .

Leland College, Baker Louisiana. (n.d.). Historic Structures. Retrieved July 23, 2022, from http://historicstructures.com/la/baker/leland_college.php

Mchie, B. (2020, May 16). *Leland College is Founded*. African American Registry. https://aaregistry.org/ story/leland-college-founded/

Our beginnings. (n.d.). St. Francisville Funeral Home. Retrieved July 24, 2022, from https://www. stfrancisvillefuneralhome.com/history

The Elders Speak: the West Feliciana Parish African American oral history project. (n.d.). Retrieved July 23, 2022, from https://www. louisianafolklife.org/LT/Articles_ Essays/WestFeliciana8.html

Thomas Dawson. (n.d.). Visual & Performing Arts. Retrieved July 24, 2022, from https://vapa.uccs.edu/ index/music/faculty/dawson

(N.d.). Retrieved July 24, 2022, from https://fzot.rnsmessina.it/sermons-by-black-preachers-free.html 1963, B. A. (n.d.). *Birth of a Voter (CORE reprint, of Ebony Magazine article).*

CORE, J. F. (n.d.). *Louisiana Story, 1963. CORE pamphlet.*

(2015, June 22). SU Ag Center chancellor Leodrey Williams to retire after half a century. HBCU Buzz. https:// hbcubuzz.com/2015/06/ su-ag-center-chancellor-leodrey-williams-to-retire-after-half-a-century/

Printed in the United States
by Baker & Taylor Publisher Services